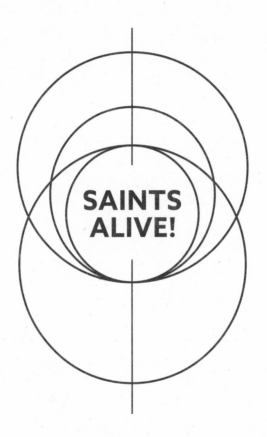

SAINTS
ALIVE!

PARTICIPANT'S JOURNAL
JOHN FINNEY & FELICITY LAWSON

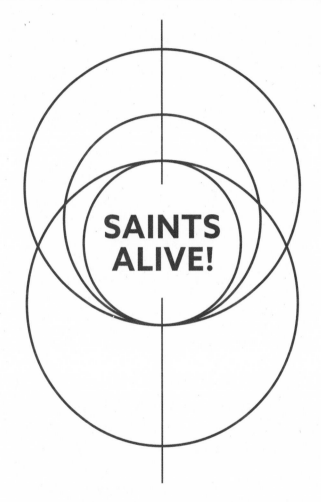

SAINTS
ALIVE!

LIVING LIFE IN THE SPIRIT TODAY
A NINE-WEEK COURSE FOR CHURCHES AND SMALL GROUPS

DAVID C COOK

transforming lives together

SAINTS ALIVE! PARTICIPANT'S JOURNAL
Published by David C Cook
4050 Lee Vance Drive
Colorado Springs, CO 80918 U.S.A.

Integrity Music Limited, a Division of David C Cook
Brighton, East Sussex BN1 2RE, England

The graphic circle C logo is a registered trademark of David C Cook.

The website addresses recommended throughout this book are offered as a
resource to you. These websites are not intended in any way to be or imply an
endorsement on the part of David C Cook, nor do we vouch for their content.

Unless otherwise noted, all Scripture references are taken from the *Holy Bible*,
New Living Translation, copyright © 1996, 2007 by Tyndale House Foundation.
Used by permission of Tyndale House Publishers, Inc., Carol Stream, Illinois
60188. All rights reserved. Scripture quotations marked PHILLIPS are taken
from The New Testament in Modern English, Revised Edition © 1972 by
J. B. Phillips. Copyright renewed © 1986, 1988 by Vera M. Phillips.

ISBN 978-0-8307-8149-2
eISBN 978-0-8307-8214-7

© 2020 John Finney and Felicity Lawson
First edition published by SPCK in 1982 © John Finney
and Felicity Lawson, ISBN 978-0-7459-3140-1

The Team: Ian Matthews, Jennie Pollock, Jack Campbell, Susan Murdock
Cover Design: Mark Prentice at beatroot.media

Printed in the United Kingdom
Third Edition 2020

1 2 3 4 5 6 7 8 9 10

100120

CONTENTS

———

INTRODUCTION

This Journal is yours. As you are part of the Saints Alive! Course, this Journal will help you get the most out of it.

Saints Alive! is for people who mean business. It is for anyone who wants to find out more about God and his power and love—and who is prepared to do something about it. No Christian knowledge is necessary, just a willingness to look for new treasures.

If You Are by Yourself

This Journal is written for people in a Saints Alive! group. However, it can be used:

- as a way of finding out about the Christian faith **by yourself**. Just ignore all the stuff about groups and carry on!
- for those who think their faith has got too complicated and want to go back to basics
- to find out how the Christian faith fits in with mindfulness and meditation

You can use it:

- as a memo to yourself—to remember what you have done;
- as a planner—to make resolutions for the future;
- for meditation—to think about who you are and what you do;
- or just for making notes.

It does not matter what your Journal looks like. It can look a mess—but it is your mess and nobody is going to look at it and say, 'Ugh'.

You can stick things in it, like coloured stars and funny illustrations. You can draw pictures and diagrams. You can write down resolutions and prayers and thoughts.

A lot of people find Journals useful to get things organised. They can make you feel better and help you to think about the future. They are also a great aid to memory.

Or you are at liberty to throw it away—after all, it is your Journal and you can do what you like with it! Though be careful—you might want to fish it out of the dustbin later when you've thought about it!

WELCOME

Welcome to the Saints Alive! course. It has been used by hundreds of thousands of people of differing denominations and in many countries. It has been used on every continent except Antarctica! It has been used in prisons and in schools, in traditional churches a thousand years old and in fellowships that have just started.

Saints Alive! is renowned for its flexibility. This is *your* course, and what you think and say (or don't say) is all-important. You are different from everybody else and your personal needs should be honoured, and your opinions taken into account.

It does not matter how much or how little you know about the Christian faith or the Bible or being a Christian. Some in your group may know absolutely nothing and have been drawn along by vague curiosity while others may just be wanting a 'refresher' because they want their faith to be more real to them. Whatever you and the rest know or don't know is immaterial: God wants to change and help all of you.

HOW TO USE THIS JOURNAL

It is divided into eight sections, which are connected with the first eight sessions of the Saints Alive! course. (The ninth session is a celebration.) There is also an Appendix with various texts, mostly from the video.

Each section has:

o Notes about the last session so that you can reflect on what was discussed

- A guide to the next bit of Chunk Reading
- Some Daily Bible Reading notes
- There is plenty of space for you:
  - To jot down any thoughts or questions you have after your group meeting
  - To note anything that strikes you as you do the Chunk Reading
  - To reflect on the questions in the Daily Reading
  - To keep a record of anything God is saying to you during the course
  - To write or draw your ideas, dreams, questions or simply put in things that appeal to you
  - At the end there are copies of scripts from the videos, which might help you remember what was said

What you write down is completely personal and private. You may find it useful to take it to group meetings. However, no one should ask to see it, and you will probably get more from the meeting if you don't have it open in front of you the whole time.

USING ONE OF

GOD'S

GREATEST GIFTS –

your imagination.

HOW DO YOU THINK?

Getting the most from this Journal can depend on the way you think!

We often assume that everyone thinks in the same way that we do. They don't.

Research shows that roughly a quarter of people think nearly always in pictures, a quarter think in words and half use a mixture of the two.

Most teachers think in words. Most engineers and architects think in pictures—and so do most inventors. Verbal thinkers think with words—it's a bit like talking to yourself in your head. Picture thinkers see 'pictures' in their heads—as though they were watching a film. Einstein thought in pictures.

In your Journal therefore some of you may find it best to use words to answer questions and to jot down your ideas. But you may be someone who thinks in pictures: you do not have to use words, and you may be at your most creative using pictures. 'A picture is worth a thousand words' is still true. A dense page of statistics can be summed up in a graph. A long description of what to do can be made into a flow-chart. An emotion can be expressed as a colour. Advertisers use far more pictures than words.

There is plenty of plain paper in your Journal to write down your thoughts in words—but also plenty to use for pictures.

Some will find the following options best:

- Use sketches—visualise a scene in the Bible. It does not require a masterpiece—pinpeople will do nicely.

o Download a picture from the internet that means something to you. Print it off and paste it in your Journal. Enter 'Jesus images' in your computer and you will have ten thousand pictures to choose from.

o When Chunk Reading the book of Acts, draw a map, or download one from the internet, to follow where the story is taking place.

o In this Journal you have some diagrams which were used to summarise ideas. Are there any diagrams you can create to show what you are thinking?

o Don't be afraid to doodle!

▼

Imagination
is a
wonderful
gift of God -

LET'S USE IT TO THE FULL.

▲

THE BIBLE

Finding Your Way Around

The Bible is divided into two parts: the Old Testament and the New Testament. Each part is divided into different books—most of them written by different authors. The books of the Old Testament come from the time before Jesus while those in the New Testament describe his life and that of the early church.

It will help you to find the books more quickly if you use the *contents page*, which is somewhere near the front. (Some books have a number before them, e.g., 1 John or 2 Peter, because there is more than one book of the same name.)

Each book is divided into chapters and verses. Some Bibles have two columns per page.

Finding a particular reading

Using the Bible

Let God speak to you through the Bible. St Augustine long ago described the Bible as 'our letters from home'. Before you begin, ask God to help you to understand what you are reading and to hear his special message for you.

Read slowly. We live in a world where we speed-read—skimming through the internet, scanning the newspapers, glancing at the adverts. Read the Bible like poetry (a lot of it is poetry!) and thoughtfully make it your own.

Some of the readings in this Journal have questions. These are to help you to understand what you are reading and to see how God's Word fits your situation. This is for your use only—no one will ask to see your answers.

The Bible was written long ago in Hebrew (the Old Testament) and Greek (the New Testament) and has been translated into nearly every language on earth. It is best to use a modern version. The Saints Alive! course and the Journal use the New Living Translation. The Anglicised edition is published by SPCK, or you can download a digital version through the YouVersion Bible app or follow it at www.bible.com or other internet websites. (If you have another version, you may find that slightly different words are used from those used in this Journal.)

Chunk Reading

Often in church we read only a few verses at a time. But that is not how the Bible was designed to be read. The Chunk Readings are to help you to read the Bible in the same way that you might read a book—quite a lot at a time. This way you get a better understanding of the whole story. Many people find this one of the most exciting and worthwhile parts of the course. One ex-miner read a whole gospel straight through and exclaimed about Jesus, 'Wow, what a man!'

These days it is easy to listen to passages of the Bible on the internet or on an app. You can listen to the New Living Translation on the YouVersion Bible app or at www.bible.com.

During this course you will be encouraged to read or listen to the gospel of Mark, the Acts of the Apostles and Paul's letter to the Philippians. By doing this, you will have read about the life and ministry of Jesus and the story of the first Christians.

You may find it helpful to plan ahead and set aside about three-quarters of an hour each week. Get comfortable and settle down to do your Chunk Reading.

Daily Readings

Many Christians find it helpful to try to read the Bible and pray every day. The Daily Readings will help you to do this. They supplement the teaching given during the course and are usually based on the previous week's session.

Try to set aside ten to fifteen minutes each day to be quiet and draw close to God. This 'Quiet Time' is best when you are not too tired. Try to find a place where you won't be interrupted. The Bible says, 'When you pray, go away by yourself, shut the door behind you, and pray to your Father in private' (Matthew 6:6). If you can't always manage every day, don't worry. Some people find it easier than others to find a regular time and get into a routine. If you are a parent with young children and/or you work shifts, it will be difficult. It is better to try to get one time in the week which is 'your own' than to feel stressed about not making it every day.

However you do it, a routine of Bible reading and prayer will help you long after Saints Alive! is finished.

PRAYER

Prayer is simply being with God and sharing ourselves with him. There is no 'correct' way to pray, but if prayer is new to you, the following points may be helpful:

- Be natural with God. Tell him what you really feel in your own words, not just what you think he wants to hear. God loves us to share ourselves with him, and our first stumbling words of prayer are as precious to him as the first words of a baby are to its parents.
- There is no need to get into a special position to pray. Some people find it helpful to kneel, but you can sit, walk or lie down. Be comfortable so that your attention can be focussed on God and not on yourself.
- It is important to have special times for prayer, but we can talk to God at any time and any place—at work, in the shops, even while having a bath. The more you pray, the more natural prayer will become.
- There are many ways of praying:

    Silence. Simply be quiet before God and soak up his presence—think of it as spiritual sunbathing (Sonbathing!). A good way to begin.

    Praise. Tell God how great he is and that you love him.

    Confession. When you know that you are in the wrong and that there has been a cloud between you and God—tell him that you are sorry and ask for help to change.

Thanksgiving. Thank God for what he has done for you and for others.

Intercession. Ask him for those things that you and others need. Try to keep a balance between praying for yourself and praying for other people and the world we live in.

Many people find it helpful to pray the Lord's Prayer as part of their daily pattern. There are several versions in use but the two most common are:

Modern	**Traditional**
Our Father in heaven,	Our Father, who art in heaven,
hallowed be your name,	hallowed be thy name;
your kingdom come,	thy kingdom come;
your will be done,	thy will be done;
on earth as in heaven.	on earth as it is in heaven.
Give us today our daily bread.	Give us this day our daily bread.
Forgive us our sins	And forgive us our trespasses,
as we forgive those who sin	as we forgive those who trespass
against us.	against us.
Lead us not into temptation	And lead us not into temptation;
but deliver us from evil.	but deliver us from evil.
For the kingdom, the power,	For thine is the kingdom,
and the glory are yours	the power and the glory,
now and for ever.	for ever and ever.
Amen.	Amen.

Another prayer which may be used at the end of your sessions is adapted from 2 Corinthians 13:14 and is known as **The Grace**.

> May the grace of our Lord Jesus
> Christ, and the love of God,
> and the fellowship of the Holy Spirit
> be with us all, now and evermore.
> Amen.

But remember that prayer is really a conversation with God. You need to leave time to listen to him as well as talk with him. If we meet up with a friend, we would want to hear what they have to say to us as well as telling them our news. It's the same with God.

Notes about the Group Meetings

- Every session is like a football match—it will last ninety minutes, but there may be 'extra time' of thirty minutes if it is needed. If you want to arrange for someone to pick you up, it is often easiest to send a text at the end of the meeting. If this is difficult, you will nearly always find someone to take you home.
- Dress: casual!
- Most people talk—but don't feel you have to.
- All discussion is good, though argument for argument's sake does not help the group.

- If you want to talk about anything private, have a quiet word with one of the leaders and you can fix a time to meet.
- People often talk very openly during group meetings. Please keep anything you hear confidential.
- Begin to pray for the other members of the group.
- If you are feeling a bit nervous or excited—you are not the only one!
- If you have any special requirements, e.g., with access, hearing or vision, or if you are a vegetarian/vegan or have food allergies, please do let your leaders know. They will want to be as welcoming to everyone as possible.

Memo

The next meetings will be:

On _____, _____, _____

At _____ a.m./p.m. and _____ a.m./p.m. and _____ a.m./p.m.

Address(s) _____

_____

_____

Contact phone number (if you want to ask a question) _____

Email _____

SPARKS

———

Every day you come across sparks.

Things happen—both good and bad—that interest you. People say things and do things that make an impact on you. TV and social media bombard you with pictures and noise. Something makes you laugh—or cry. Your Saints Alive! group will produce stories, quotations, jokes, Bible verses, prayers and ideas.

We all have 'Aha' moments. Like sparks from a bonfire they fly up into the sky. Some you can catch and put down in your Journal in words or pictures.

Then you can use these to spark off ideas of your own. If you find one, put it down before the spark goes out. Memory is short—sketch that picture, write that story, put that idea into practice before the spark is gone.

If something striking happens—put it down. If you come across a quotation that speaks to you—put it down. If a story makes you think—put it down. If you see a picture in a magazine or on a card that speaks to you—stick it in.

These are for dipping into at any time.

The best sparks are those you catch, and that set off a train of ideas and decisions for you.

'Good Lord, may my eyes see what is important and my ears hear what is valuable, so that I may learn to see you in all things and may do what is right.'

That's what your Journal is for—to enjoy ... enlarge ... enthuse.

RELATIONSHIPS MATTER

———

Summary of the Session

In this first session you will have had the opportunity, if you have not done so before, to meet your leaders and fellow group members. Perhaps you would like to jot down any of their names that you can remember to help you next time you meet. Most will be feeling a mixture of anticipation and anxiety as the course begins. Why not pray for them?

Your group leaders will have reminded you of some of the things said at the Introductory Meeting, especially:

- No prior knowledge is expected. No contribution will be thought silly. Please do ask questions.
- You don't have to say anything unless you want to.
- Please keep personal things shared within the group confidential.

Relationships

We all have a network of relationships, some with people we are close to and others with those we don't know so well. These can bring us both joy and pain.

The quality of our relationships varies—not least within families. Some sisters and brothers get on well, but others don't! Work relationships may be supportive or destructive. Some relationships will be deeper or more superficial than others.

Time also matters. Lovers do not always love forever.

When relationships are positive we probably feel:

- good about ourselves;
- valued/supported;
- able to grow and try new things.

When relationships are poor we may feel:

- without worth/unloved;
- angry;
- anxious/bitter;
- unable to reach our full potential.

Relationships can end when:

- there is an almighty quarrel with anger and slammed doors;
- people drift apart without realising it;
- other relationships take priority;
- people develop different interests;
- people have different aims and priorities;
- people get bored with each other.

A Relationship with God

The Bible and Christian experience down the centuries tells us that, amazing as it may seem, God wants a relationship with us. God created us and loves us. Loving relationships are at the very heart of God, whom Christians know as Father, Son and Holy Spirit.

Jesus prayed to God as Father. Not everyone has a good relationship with their parents, but we all know what is involved in good parenting. For example: appropriate care as we grow up; stability; food and warmth; love; discipline and forgiveness; freedom to grow and be ourselves.

The other side to this is what we think an ideal child should give to their parents. For example: love, helpfulness, trust.

If children are unsure of the love of a parent they may try to 'buy' their love by

- slaving round the house;
- over-working at school;

- being strangely well-behaved,

or they rebel against their parents and

- have temper tantrums;
- go their own way;
- are deliberately disobedient.

Neither is good. The first leads to a worried, over-conscientious person and the second to an adult who finds it difficult to trust others or make deep relationships.

Often a poor relationship with our parents can be one of the factors that influences the way we see God.

How Do People Think of God?

Some people may see 'God' as

- identified with creation;
- a benevolent old-man-in-the-sky;
- an autocrat who makes demands—a policeman or head teacher who keeps accounts of wrongs;
- one among many—as in some religions;
- a generalised force for good;
- an impersonal spirit—as in much New Age thinking;
- 'something out there that has influence over my life'— through the stars, crystals, extra-terrestrials, hexing, etc.;

- non-existent;
- a figment of people's imagination—for those who need a prop in life.

The Bible speaks of God as a person who wants a relationship with human beings and is continually reaching out to them in love. Christians believe that Jesus shows us what God is like. We shall be thinking a bit more about that next week.

God the Father has all that we look for in an ideal parent and much, much more. But we can behave like children trying to earn their parents' favour by giving presents to our heavenly Father, e.g., going to church or living a 'good' life.

Our capacity to want to do our own thing means our relationship with God breaks down in very similar ways to human relationships breaking down:

- Perhaps we have never had a relationship with God because of our upbringing.
- An episode where we feel God has let us down or wasn't there when we needed him leads to anger and rejection.
- We drift apart from God without realising it.
- Other relationships become more important—Christian fellowship takes second place.
- We develop different interests—the church no longer has any attraction for us.
- We choose different values—in defiance of God.

- We feel bored with God—there seems no spice in living as a Christian.
- Believing in God is no longer 'cool'—as for many teenagers.
- Life becomes busy—demanding job/young family, etc.

Jesus told a well-known story that speaks about God's longing to have a relationship with us. You can read the story of The Two Sons in Luke 15:11-24. The video script of The Two Sons can be found on page 150 at the back of this Journal.

Your group leaders may have asked some or all of these questions about this story:

1. Who do you identify with—the loving father, the younger brother, who has come to his senses, or the resentful older brother?

2. If we identify the father with God the Father, what does that tell us about God and his relationship with us?

3. Has there ever been a time when you 'came to your senses' and started to change your life around?

4. St Augustine said, 'You [God] have made us for yourself and our hearts are restless until they find their rest in you'. Have you ever known that sense of restlessness, of searching for something or someone even if you don't know what/who it is?

5. The father accepted both of the brothers because they were part of his family, whatever they had, or had not,

done. The Bible talks of God's love being completely certain and absolutely unconditional.

Loving and Being Loved

Loving relationships make an impact on our lives. Think of falling in love with someone. The Andrew Lloyd Webber song 'Love Changes Everything' encapsulates this.

Some change happens naturally. Other people often notice the change when people fall in love. Knowing you are loved makes you feel better about yourself. You want to do things to show your love for the other person. You think about what the other person feels or needs. But as the relationship grows, some changes have to be worked at because none of us is perfect and our broken bits can annoy or hurt the other person. In a truly loving relationship, people grow and fulfil more of their potential.

Jesus said, 'My purpose is to give [you] a rich and satisfying life' (John 10:10). Because God loves us, he wants us to be more and more the people he created us to be.

The prayer of the leaders is that during the course each person (including the leaders) will grow in their relationship with God, whether you have been a Christian for years or whether at this point you are not even sure that God exists. He will work in each one of us differently because each one of us is unique. Each of us is at a different stage of our lives and in our Christian journey. But for each of us, this will mean change. Change is not something we need to be frightened about, for this is change for the better.

Change is part of life, and what doesn't change is dead. If you are alive, you change!

At the end of the session you will probably have taken part in a short meditation about a cottage. You can find the script on page 152 at the end of this Journal.

Thinking Back over This Session

If you would like to, jot down here any thoughts or questions you have about this week's session:

CHUNK READING

In church we often read only short passages from the Bible, though its contents were not written to be read in that way. An important part of Saints Alive! is the Chunk Reading, which allows us to see the bigger picture. If you prefer to listen to rather than read these passages, then the YouVersion app, which we recommend, has an audio option so you can listen to passages from the New Living Translation. None of the Chunks we recommend should take longer than thirty minutes to read.

The first four books in the New Testament are known as Gospels—Matthew, Mark, Luke and John. They all tell the story of the life, teaching and ministry of Jesus. They are not biographies or histories as we understand them today. They don't set out to tell us everything there is to know about Jesus, though scholarly research has shown that they are historically reliable. They were written to pass on the story of Jesus so that the first Christians could be strengthened and grow in their faith and so that enquirers could discover for themselves who Jesus is and what he taught.

Matthew, Mark and Luke have much material in common with one another. John's approach and style of writing is rather different. Mark is the shortest of the Gospels, and many people think it was the first to be written. We have chosen to begin our Chunk Reading with Mark. Some of the daily readings will help you dip into the other Gospels and different parts of the Bible.

This week's Chunk is Mark Chapters 1-8.

Try to read it through, or listen to it, in one sitting. Have two questions in your mind as you do so:

- o What sort of person was Jesus?
- o What kind of things did he do?

You might like to jot down or draw some of your thoughts in this space as we shall be thinking about these questions in Session 2. (Don't worry though, no one will put you on the spot to give an answer!)

DAILY BIBLE READINGS

Seek the Kingdom of God above all else, and he will give you everything you need. (Luke 12:31)

Day 1

The Bible tells us that God loves each one of us and that he wants us to know him and trust him as the very best of Fathers. Jesus came to show us what God is like and to make it possible for us to know him and experience his love.

Read what John says about Jesus in **John 1:10-14**. What strikes you about these few verses?

Spend a few minutes thanking God for his love and asking that you may come to know him better.

Day 2

Jesus spent much of his time with the ordinary people who often felt that God didn't love or care about them. Indeed, some of the religious leaders looked down on them and criticised them and called them sinners. In the first session we thought about the story of The Two Sons in Luke's gospel. Jesus told two more stories about things that were lost in

Luke 15:3-10. How do you think the ordinary people would have felt when they heard him tell these stories?

How do you think God feels about you?

Day 3

John the Baptist was sent by God to prepare the way for Jesus by his preaching and by baptising people in the river Jordan. One day John pointed out Jesus to two of his followers, who followed Jesus wanting to find out more. You can read about this in **John 1:35-39**. Jesus invited them to 'Come and see'. It was the beginning of a big adventure for those first disciples of Jesus. Being on the Saints Alive! course is an opportunity to come and discover more about Jesus for ourselves.

Are you just at the beginning of your journey, or have you been following him for some time? How do you feel about his invitation to 'come and see'?

Day 4

Zacchaeus was someone who was curious about Jesus. He had heard about him, and when Jesus came to town he wanted to see him. He went to extraordinary lengths to do so. You can read his story in **Luke 19:1-10**. What things strike you as important about this story?

Day 5

Another story Jesus tells is of two sisters who were friends of Jesus. Their names were Martha and Mary. You can read their story in **Luke 10:38-48**. Most of us have more than a little sympathy with Martha. Our lives tend to be very full of things we need to do. (Or things we *think* we need to do!) Why do you think that Jesus says to Martha that her sister has made the right choice?

Is God saying anything to you through this story about the choices you make?

Day 6

Today we are going to delve into the middle of the Old Testament
and look at **Psalm 63:1-8**. It speaks of one person's longing for God.
Can you identify with the writer? Can you echo his words? Try saying
the verses through again as if you are saying them to God.

Perhaps you could write a psalm or prayer expressing your longing for God. Or perhaps you want to say to God that you don't feel
like the psalmist.

Day 7

One of the best known passages in the Bible is **Psalm 23**. It may have
been written by David, who was a shepherd before he became King
of Israel. It speaks of God's provision, guidance and protection. Are
there ways in which this psalm speaks to you? Can you think of a
time when you felt that God provided in some way for your needs?

Or guided you in a decision you had to make? Or protected you in some way, even if at the time you did not realise it might be God?

Pray today for the next group meeting and for all who will be there, that everyone will grow in their understanding of who Jesus is and what he has done for us.

Journal Pages

Lord Jesus, I don't know much about
you, but I am willing to learn;
and I am ready to give all that I know
of myself to all that I know of you;
and I am willing to go on learning.

Donald Coggan

Journal Pages

Almighty God,
give us the wisdom to perceive you,
intellect to understand you,
diligence to seek you,
patience to wait for you,
eyes to behold you,
a heart to meditate upon you
and a life to proclaim you,
through the power of the Spirit of
  our Lord Jesus Christ.

St Benedict (480-543)

Journal Pages

THE BEATITUDES

God blesses those who are poor and realize
their need for him,
for the Kingdom of Heaven is theirs.
God blesses those who mourn,
for they will be comforted.
God blesses those who are humble,
for they will inherit the whole earth.
God blesses those who hunger and thirst
for justice,
for they will be satisfied.
God blesses those who are merciful,
for they will be shown mercy.
God blesses those whose hearts are pure,
for they will see God.
God blesses those who work for peace,
for they will be called the children of God.
God blesses those who are persecuted for
doing right,
for the Kingdom of Heaven is theirs.

(Matthew 5:3-10)

SESSION 2

WHO IS JESUS?

——

The Person of Jesus

The Chunk Reading of Mark 1-8 asked, 'What sort of person is Jesus and what kind of things did he do?' Your group will have put together a 'word portrait' of Jesus. What struck you as most important about that portrait?

You may have noticed his humanity as well as the signs of his divinity. Jesus shows us what it means to be truly human as well as showing us what God is like. Because he is fully human, people can identify with him and, very importantly, he knows how we feel. He has been through the whole range of human experience so there is nothing we can go through in life that he cannot understand.

Jesus began his public ministry when he was anointed with the Holy Spirit at his baptism. Mark thinks this is so significant he begins his gospel at this point and doesn't record anything about the birth of Jesus.

Who Is He?

In Mark 8:27-33 we read about the time when Jesus asked his disciples who other people thought he was. Then he asked them who they thought he was. There comes a point when all of us have to answer that question.

'The people' are looking at important people from the past, trying to find a model that would fit. (Elijah was an important Old Testament prophet, and John the Baptist had recently been beheaded by Herod.) Peter correctly identifies Jesus as the promised Messiah, the one who would set the Jewish people free. But Jesus was not the kind of Messiah the Jews were expecting—a military and political liberator or a supernatural wonder worker. He had rejected these models at his temptations.

Even Peter couldn't understand what Jesus was saying about what it would mean for him to be the Messiah. Jesus' understanding of his calling was shaped by the passages in Isaiah about the Suffering Servant, whose path to glory is the way of suffering. And for Jesus, of course, that meant the way of the cross.

The Passion

The rest of this session focused on the last week of Jesus' life—what is often called 'The Passion'. There are lots more things you could have looked at like the 'I am' sayings in John's gospel, but Christians believe the events of this last week are so important that we left plenty of time to reflect on them.

Even in church we often don't hear how the whole week fits together. 'The Message of the Cross' from the video is based round still pictures depicting the events of that week with the narrative based on passages from the Gospels. You can read the text of the video on page 153 at the back of this Journal. It might help you relive some of the special moments in the video for you.

The Importance of Response

At the end of the video we are reminded that there are various responses we can make to the death of Jesus. The one thing we cannot do is nothing—that in itself is rejection, for to ignore someone is to reject them.

The New Testament describes a Christian as someone who is 'in Christ'—someone for whom Jesus is Lord of their life. To be a Christian is to acknowledge that Jesus died for our sins so that we might be forgiven and put back into a right relationship with God. That is the symbolism of the curtain in the Temple being torn in two. (This curtain separated the Holy of Holies, which symbolised the very presence of God himself, from the rest of the Temple. No one could enter except the High Priest once a year. The death of Jesus opens the way for everyone who wants to have a relationship with God to do so.)

There are different ways in which human beings can relate to God. A simple visual aid was used to explain this:

1. The first big circle represents our lives. In the circle there are a series of smaller circles representing different aspects of our lives, e.g., F = Family, W = Work, R = Relationships and friendships, L = Leisure activities. The 'I' in the centre of this circle represents the life without God where 'I' decide what I will do. The cross is outside because **for some people it is as if Jesus is right outside their lives.**

2. The second circle is identical to the first but with a faint dotted cross in it. This represents the life where the knowledge and experience of Jesus is only a faint memory. **This is the nostalgic Christian.**

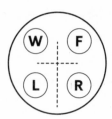

3. The third circle is identical to the first but contains a small circle with a cross in it. This represents a life where the Christian faith, prayer and even going to church is important but where the individual remains firmly in control. Faith is essentially one interest among many, and there may be some areas in the person's life where they do not welcome God or Christian values. Jesus is important but is in a 'compartment'. **The restricted Christian.**

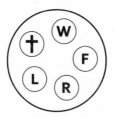

4. In the fourth circle the central 'I' has been replaced by the cross. It is on the cross that Jesus shows us the full extent of his love. It is only as we know ourselves to be loved totally and unconditionally that we can give ourselves to this amazing God and allow Jesus to be the centre of our lives. He is our Lord and influences every aspect of our being—our attitudes to work, our relationships, our political opinions, how we spend our leisure, etc. This is what Jesus died to achieve, for it is only when he is at the centre of our lives as Lord that we are truly ourselves, truly the people God created us to

be. We know that God loves us, really loves us, and this sets us free from having to achieve or do or be anything to get his approval. This is at the heart of what it means to be **a Christian disciple.**

Is there a circle that you identify with?

Even once we have surrendered our lives to God in Christ, we do not always live fully in the fourth circle. That's why as Christians we offer our lives afresh to God each day, repent of the things that draw us away from him and ask for his grace to follow Jesus faithfully.

Thinking Back over This Session

If you would like to, jot down here any thoughts or questions you have about this week's session:

CHUNK READING

This week the Chunk Reading continues with the second half of Mark's gospel. Last week finished with chapter 8, where Jesus asks his disciples to consider who he really is and what this means. This week begins with what we call the Transfiguration, where we get a glimpse into his identity as the Son of God and the purpose for which he came to earth. Moses and Elijah represent the Old Testament Law and Prophets. Jesus came as the fulfilment of all that is promised in the Old Testament.

Read **Mark chapters 9-16**. This week's Chunk Reading ends with the story of the cross. As you read it, let two thoughts be in your mind:

- The people who crucified Jesus were not terrible people. They were ordinary people who, out of fear and self-concern, destroyed the only perfect, innocent human being who has ever lived. Many probably thought they were doing the right thing.
- How much Jesus must love us to go through that for us.

DAILY READINGS

> God showed how much he loved us by sending his one
> and only Son into the world so that we might have
> eternal life through him. This is real love—not that we
> loved God, but that he loved us and sent his Son as a
> sacrifice to take away our sins. (1 John 4:9-10)

Day 1

In his first letter, John explains to his readers what the cross is all
about. Read **1 John 4:9-12**. *(John's three letters come at the end of the
New Testament, not near his gospel, which is at the beginning. Use the
contents list in your Bible to help you find them.)*

Why did God send Jesus? How does John suggest we should
respond?

Day 2

Many centuries before Jesus, the prophet Isaiah in the Old Testament
foretold that the chosen servant of God would suffer for the sins of
the people. The Suffering Servant passages were very important for
Jesus as he thought about his calling. The longest of these passages,
Isaiah 52:13-53:12, contains many remarkable parallels with what
actually happened to Jesus. What answers does Isaiah give to these
questions:

- ○ Why did Jesus die?
- ○ What was the result of his death?

Day 3

Last week we read Psalm 23 about the care and provision of the Lord, who is our shepherd. In **John 10:11-18** Jesus says to his disciples that he is the Good Shepherd. What strikes you as important about this passage? Can you think of a time in your life when God/Jesus was like a shepherd to you?

Day 4

The first Christians quickly came to recognise that Jesus was more than just a good man. Writing some years after the crucifixion and resurrection of Jesus, Paul speaks of the full grandeur of Christ. Read **Colossians 1:15-22**. What does this passage tell us about:

- who Jesus is?
- what he has achieved for us?

Day 5

On the day of Pentecost, Peter spoke to the crowds about Jesus. Read **Acts 2:22-24** and **32-39**.

- What did he say about the death of Jesus (v. 23)?
- What did God do (vv. 24, 32-33, 36)?
- What did Peter tell them to do in order to receive God's promise of forgiveness and the Holy Spirit (vv. 38-39)?

Day 6

Revelation, the last book in the Bible, is not easy to understand, but in the first three chapters John records messages from Jesus to some of the first churches. **Revelation 3:20** gives us a simple picture of how Jesus is waiting for us to respond to him and invite him right into the centre of our lives. These words were originally addressed to Christians whose love for Jesus had grown cold, like in the second circle of last week's session. But they can equally be applied to people who have never before asked him to be Lord of their lives. Either way, this is the same message as the fourth circle in this week's session.

- o What promise does Jesus give to those who open the door?

Day 7

In **John 6:35-40** Jesus makes three promises to those who come to him. What are they?

Pray especially today for your next session and ask that everyone may grow in their understanding of the resurrection of Jesus.

Journal Pages

Thanks be to you, Lord Jesus Christ,
for all the benefits you have won for us,
for all the pains and insults you have
  borne for us.
O most merciful Redeemer, Friend and
  Brother,
may we know you more clearly,
love you more dearly,
and follow you more nearly,
day by day.

Richard of Chichester (1197-1253)

Journal Pages

Were you there when they
   crucified my Lord?
Were you there when they
   crucified my Lord?
O sometimes it causes me to
   tremble! tremble! tremble!
Were you there when they
   crucified my Lord?

African American Spiritual

SESSION 3

THE RESURRECTION

——

The First Easter Day

The session began with the account of Mary Magdalene in the garden on the video. The disciples were incredulous! After all, it was only on Friday that they had watched Jesus being crucified. They were still in shock and disbelief that he was dead. They would have been feeling a mixture of confusion, anger, numbness and fear for themselves.

Luke 24:13-24

The setting is Easter day. Cleopas and his companion were followers of Jesus but not members of the Twelve. They had been in Jerusalem for the Passover, but we don't know whether they witnessed the crucifixion or only heard about it from those who were there. They had clearly been with the Twelve and other disciples as the events of Easter day unfolded.

Notice the conversation Cleopas and his companion were having and how they were feeling. They may well have been going over and over the events that had taken place and asking 'Why?'

What impact had the reports of the women and the others who had been to the tomb have on them?

They were not expecting to see Jesus, so it is not surprising they didn't recognise him when he drew alongside them.

Jesus asked them what they were talking about because they needed to talk and tell him their story.

Luke 24:25-32

In vv. 25-27 Jesus is giving them a new perspective. Helping them to see that the crucifixion wasn't a terrible mistake but part of God's plan.

Now look at vv. 28-29. Why do you think that Jesus walked ahead 'as if he were going on'? What made them invite him to stay? Perhaps Jesus acted as if he were going on because he was waiting for their invitation. Jesus never forces himself on anyone; he waits until they are ready to take the next step of faith.

Now consider vv. 30-32. They recognised him—they suddenly saw that he was Jesus. This was a moment of revelation, of spiritual insight. So far as we know, these two disciples were not at the Last Supper, where Jesus had broken bread with his disciples on the night before he died, so it was not simply a sparking of memory. Have you experienced any eye-opening moments? Notice how they had felt while Jesus was talking with them on the road. Have you had that sense of excitement during this course so far?

Luke 24:33-43

The reaction of Cleopas and his companion is to rush back to Jerusalem to tell their friends the good news that Jesus is alive. When they get there, they discover that the amazing news has got there before them because Jesus has also appeared to Peter.

Not surprisingly the events of the first Easter day are hard to piece together. Each gospel tells the story slightly differently. This is part of their authenticity, reflecting that they are eyewitness accounts with different people remembering different parts depending on their personal involvement, and then passing their memories on to those who wrote the Gospels. The gospel writers then selected from those memories the aspects of the many different resurrection appearances that fitted best with their particular telling of the story of Jesus.

In Luke 24:36-43 you can see the fear of the disciples who thought they had seen a ghost, despite having just been told that Jesus had appeared to Peter and the two disciples on the road. They are invited to touch his wounds, as is Thomas in John 20:27. Jesus eats to prove they are not seeing a ghost.

Easter Day and Other Resurrection Appearances

We can be fairly certain that the following happened on the first Easter day, though we may not be sure about the precise order:

- The women go to the tomb and find the stone rolled away and the tomb empty. They see a vision of angels who tell them Jesus is alive (all four gospels).
- Peter and John go to investigate but don't see Jesus (John 20:2-10; Luke 24:24).
- Mary meets Jesus in the garden (John 20:11-18).
- Peter sees the risen Jesus (Luke 24:34).
- Jesus appears to the two disciples on the Emmaus Road (Luke 24:13-35).
- Jesus appears to a group of disciples (Luke 24:36-43; John 20:19-23).

We also have accounts of other resurrection appearances:

- Jesus appearing in the upper room and speaking with Thomas (John 20:24-29).
- Jesus appearing with the disciples in Galilee (Matthew 28:10, 16-20; John 21:1-23).
- In 1 Corinthians 15:5-7, Paul gives his summary of the resurrection appearances as he had heard about them, including one occasion when Jesus appeared to over 500 of his followers at once.

If you would like to read about the evidence for the resurrection of Jesus, you can do so on page 161 at the back of this Journal.

The Significance of the Resurrection

The resurrection is important because:

- It is God's confirmation that Jesus is who he said he
  was. The cross and resurrection were at the very heart
  of his plan of salvation.
- If Jesus is alive, we can know him today. Although not
  many people encounter the risen Christ as Paul did on
  the Damascus Road (you will find the story in Acts 9,
  which is part of the Chunk Reading for the next session), many down the ages and today have seen visions
  of him, and Christian testimony is that we know Jesus is
  alive because we have a personal relationship with him.
- Because of the death and resurrection of Jesus, we can
  know forgiveness and new beginnings.
- Paul tells us in 1 Corinthians 15 and elsewhere that
  because Jesus is alive, we can be confident that those
  who are 'in Christ' and have a relationship with him will
  also be raised from the dead. Death has been defeated.
- Paul also tells us that the resurrection of Jesus is the
  proof that evil was defeated at the cross. Although
  we still see evil at work in this world and experience
  temptation in our own lives, the resurrection assures us
  that Jesus has conquered all the powers of darkness and
  Satan is a defeated enemy.

Luke 24:44-53

Jesus could not remain forever with his disciples, appearing to them from time to time. His plans were for something far bigger than that. His plans encompassed the whole world, beginning with the disciples in Jerusalem. While he had been with them on earth, he had taught them about the gift of the Holy Spirit, whom he said the Father would send on them to equip them for this task. We shall be thinking more about the work of the Holy Spirit next week and some of the daily readings will help prepare us to do that.

Our Chunk Reading this week is from the Acts of the Apostles (often just called 'Acts'), and it begins with Luke retelling the story with which he ended his gospel, the story we have just read. In both, Jesus tells his disciples that he has a job for them to do but they must wait in Jerusalem until they receive the gift of the Holy Spirit. Then in a mysterious way he is taken from them and the chapter of his earthly life is ended. But not, of course, his work, the next chapter of which is about to begin.

Thinking Back over This Session

If you would like to, jot down here any thoughts or questions you have about this week's session:

CHUNK READING

This week we move on from reading about the earthly life of Jesus as recorded in the Gospels to the Acts of the Apostles.

Acts was written by Luke as a follow-up to his gospel. He refers back to this in the first few verses of chapter 1. Acts is the story of the early church and shows how the good news of Jesus spread from Jerusalem to the Gentile world and eventually to Rome. It focuses on the ministries of Peter and then of Paul.

The book has sometimes been called the 'Acts of the Holy Spirit' because the account of the coming of the Holy Spirit on the day of Pentecost is the springboard for the rest of the book, and Luke emphasises the work of the Holy Spirit throughout. Doctor Luke was a companion of Paul and experienced first-hand some of the events he wrote about. (You can tell which bits these were because from chapter 16 he begins to speak of 'we' instead of 'they'.)

Read **Acts chapters 1-5**. As you do so, notice

- the references to the work of the Holy Spirit among the disciples;
- what happened on the day of Pentecost;
- the part that miraculous happenings played in the everyday lives of the disciples. Such things were obviously regarded as fairly normal, just as they had been in the ministry of Jesus.

DAILY READINGS

> All praise to God, the Father of our Lord Jesus Christ. It is
> by his great mercy that we have been born again, because
> God raised Jesus Christ from the dead. (1 Peter 1:3)

Day 1

Not everyone found it easy to believe that Jesus really had been raised
from the dead. In fact, most of the disciples found it difficult even
when their close friends said they had seen him. You can read about
one of them, Thomas, in **John 20:24-29**. Do you sometimes feel a
bit like Thomas? How did Thomas respond? What did Jesus say to
Thomas that is important for us?

Day 2

In **1 Corinthians 15:1-8**, Paul reminds the Christians at Corinth of
the good news that he had preached to them. There are three things
that he says are of the greatest importance. Discover what these are in
verses 3 and 4, write them down and then give thanks for them. He
then goes on to record some of the resurrection appearances.

Day 3

Some of the Christians in Corinth were confused about the impli-
cations of the resurrection. In **1 Corinthians 15:20**, Paul reassures
them that because Jesus was raised from the dead, those who trust in
him will also experience resurrection. Paul's teaching in this chapter
is not easy to follow, but in **verses 35-37** he gives an analogy to help
them understand that there is both continuity and change between
our earthly bodies and our heavenly bodies. Do you find the analogy
of the seed and the plant that comes from it helpful?

Day 4

Because Jesus has been raised from the dead, we can experience
something of his risen life here and now. Sin need no longer have
the power over us that it once did. In **Colossians 3:1-17**, Paul uses
the idea of taking off one set of clothes and putting on another
to show the difference between the old life before we believed in
Jesus and the new life he gives us when we put our trust in him.
Although some people experience a remarkable change when they
become Christians, none of us are made perfect overnight. We need
to co-operate with God's transforming power, just as Paul urged the
Colossians to do. Are there particular things in your life that you

would like to 'take off' with the help of God? Why not talk to him about these things now?

Day 5

Look again at **Luke 24:45-53,** which we looked at together in the last session. You might like to compare it with Luke's parallel account in **Acts 1:1-9,** which is the beginning of this week's Chunk Reading. Before Jesus returns to his Father, he makes the disciples a promise and tells them what to do. You might like to make a note here of his promise and his instructions.

Day 6

Matthew also records Jesus' final meeting with his disciples before his ascension in **Matthew 28:16-20.** What are his instructions, and what promise does he make in this passage?

Day 7

Jesus did not expect his disciples to 'go into all the world and preach the gospel' unaided. He promised someone to help them, the Holy Spirit. Read **John 14:15-17; 14:25-26 and 15:26-27**. What do these verses teach us about the Holy Spirit?

In the next group meeting we shall be thinking about the work of the Holy Spirit in the lives of individuals and the church. Some of the ideas may be new to you or other members of the group. Pray that the Holy Spirit will give you understanding and a desire to experience more of his power in your lives. If you have time, you might like to go back and read again Acts 2 from this week's Chunk Reading.

Journal Pages

I also pray that you will understand the incredible greatness of God's power for us who believe him. This is the same mighty power that raised Christ from the dead and seated him in the place of honour at God's right hand in the heavenly realms. Now he is far above any ruler or authority or power or leader or anything else—not only in this world but also in the world to come. God has put all things under the authority of Christ and has made him head over all things for the benefit of the church.

(Ephesians 1:19-22)

Journal Pages

Lead us from death to life,
From falsehood to truth.
Lead us from despair to hope,
From fear to trust.
Lead us from hate to love,
From war to peace.
Let peace fill our hearts,
Our world, our universe.

World Peace Prayer

WHO IS THE HOLY SPIRIT?

———

Introduction

Acts begins where we left off last week.

- o Jesus appeared to his disciples at different times and places and continued teaching them about his mission and the task he was leaving for them to do.
- o He reminded them that they would not have to continue his work in their own strength. Just as he had been filled with the Holy Spirt at his baptism and equipped for his public ministry, so they too would be filled with the Holy Spirit.
- o They were to wait in Jerusalem until they had received this special gift (Acts 1:4-5).

○ The Holy Spirit would enable them to tell people about Jesus, starting from Jerusalem and extending throughout the known world (Acts 1:8).

○ After Jesus had left them, they returned to Jerusalem and met regularly for prayer with other disciples, including Mary and several other women (Acts 1:14).

○ They chose someone to take the place of Judas who had betrayed Jesus. Twelve was a very significant number for the Jews because there were twelve tribes of Israel, and it was no accident that Jesus had originally chosen twelve disciples to be particularly close to him and travel with him. Choosing Matthias by lot would not have seemed as strange to them as it does to us. We know very little about what happened to any of the Twelve except Peter and John. From chapter 13, Acts focuses on Paul and his companions as they take the good news of Jesus to the Gentile world.

The Day of Pentecost

Pentecost was one of the major Jewish harvest festivals, and there would have been large crowds of pilgrims in Jerusalem from all around the Mediterranean.

On the day of Pentecost:

○ Something dramatic happened that the disciples could only describe as being 'like' wind and fire. (Often we can only use picture language when trying to describe spiritual experience.)

o Each one of them was filled with the Holy Spirit, not just the Twelve.

o They began to speak in other languages. This is sometimes known as the gift of tongues. At Pentecost it was a gift that enabled them to both praise God and communicate with the crowds.

o A crowd gathered to find out what was going on. They were amazed and confused. They had never seen anything like it before. There was such an uproar that some people thought they must be drunk!

o The believers were speaking about the wonderful things God had done.

o Peter, who only a few weeks before had been afraid to admit to a slave girl that he even knew Jesus, came forward and addressed the potentially hostile crowd with confidence and authority.

Peter spoke to the crowd. In Acts we have only a summary of what he said:

o He said that what had happened was predicted in the Old Testament by the prophet Joel. God had poured out his Spirit on everyone, not just special people (2:17-18, 21).

o He talked about Jesus and how God had worked through him (v. 22).

- He explained that it was part of God's plan that Jesus should be crucified and raised back to life, and that both the Jews and the Gentiles were responsible for his death (vv. 23-24).

- He said that Jesus was the Messiah the Jews had been waiting for (vv. 25-31).

- He said that God had raised Jesus from the dead, that they could witness to this because they had met with him and that Jesus was now exalted to the place of honour at God's right hand (2:32-36). And he said that it was from there that Jesus had poured out his Holy Spirit (v. 35).

In Acts 2:37-41 we read about what happened next:

- The crowds were deeply moved and wanted to know how to respond.

- Peter said each person must take responsibility for themselves, repent, turn to God and be baptised for the forgiveness of their sins.

- He promised that they too would receive the Holy Spirit.

- He went on speaking and pressing home his point.

- About 3,000 people responded and were baptised!

In Acts 2:42-47 we read about the first Christian community:

- They were very committed to learning more; sharing with one another in fellowship, food and the Lord's

Supper (i.e., what we often call Holy Communion); and praying together (v. 42).

o The miraculous was normal, as it had been in the ministry of Jesus (v. 43).

o They shared their possessions (v. 45).

o They worshipped together in the Temple and in homes (v. 46).

o Their characteristic was joy and generosity (v. 46).

o They were well thought of and grew day by day as God added to their number (v. 47).

The Spirit Today

The Holy Spirit was not just given to the first disciples. Jesus promised to give the Holy Spirit to all who believe in him. He still gives the Holy Spirit to people who believe in him today.

At this point in the session, the group leaders will have shared the difference the Holy Spirit makes to our lives and our faith, and you may have seen some testimonies on the video. The Holy Spirit is God's gift and is given as God chooses but is freely available for all. There is no one blueprint that is followed by everyone. Some people have a dramatic and life-changing experience of being filled with the Holy Spirit, but for many others the experience is very quiet and the changes more gradual. It is the surrender to God that lies at the heart of being filled with the Spirit that is most important.

As we look at the New Testament and the experience of Christians through the ages, we discover certain common characteristics of being filled with the Spirit:

- When we ask God to fill us with his Holy Spirit, **something definite takes place.** For the first disciples it meant an overwhelming experience that could only be described as 'wind' and 'fire'. For some other people it may be far less dramatic. Nevertheless, God longs to give us this gift and always responds when we ask him. No two people's experience will ever be exactly the same. God deals with each of us differently as he knows what is best for each one of us.

- When we are filled with the Spirit, **we will change.**

- It may be that like Peter on the day of Pentecost, we find we have a **new confidence to speak about Jesus.** All of us will grow in our faith and assurance of God's love.

- For all of us the Holy Spirit begins to make us more like Jesus. Paul calls this **the fruit of the Holy Spirit**, and we shall think a bit more about this next week.

- We will be equipped to serve God and other people through the different **gifts of the Holy Spirit.** Again, more about this next week.

- Just like the first believers on the day of Pentecost, we will find ourselves **drawn towards other Christians** in worship, sharing and prayer. This togetherness is called fellowship.

- Just like those first Christians, we will find **a growing hunger to learn** more about God through studying the Scriptures and through prayer.

A Note about Tongues

For some people on Saints Alive!, speaking in tongues, one of the gifts of the Spirit mentioned at Pentecost, may be something new. The following points may have been made in the session:

- Praying in tongues is as much under our control as if we were praying in English.
- We don't have to be in an emotionally or spiritually exalted state to speak in tongues.
- It is a prayer language and is used in several ways: to praise God; to intercede for others; with the gift of interpretation to convey God's message in a particular situation; and very occasionally to speak directly to people in their own language. Although sometimes used publicly, it is most often used in private prayer.
- We don't understand it, unless it is interpreted, but it does us good!

Thinking Back over This Session

If you would like to, jot down here any thoughts or questions you have about this week's session:

CHUNK READING

Read **Acts 6-12**. (You may want to skip 7:1-50 which is hard to follow if you don't know much about the Old Testament.)

The church began in Jerusalem but, following the persecution that began with the death of Stephen, Christians were scattered throughout the region and further afield to other places where there were Jews. Wherever they went, they spoke about Jesus.

In Acts 9 we read about the conversion of Saul of Tarsus, later known as Paul. He was one of the most influential Christian missionaries, teachers and leaders of all time. It was Paul who wrote many of the letters that are preserved in the New Testament, often to churches he had founded.

In chapters 10–11 we read about the conversion of Cornelius and his household. Although he was a God-fearer (someone who worshipped in the Jewish synagogue), he was a Gentile (i.e., not a Jew). As you will see from this story, Jews and Gentiles did not normally mix, so here we have a marvellous example of the good news of Jesus leaping over racial and cultural barriers. It was so challenging to most Jewish believers that it is not surprising that Peter was called to account for his actions when he returned to Jerusalem. Although God used Peter, it was the outpouring of the Holy Spirit, just as on the day of Pentecost, that really convinced everyone.

Next week we shall be thinking about the fruit and gifts of the Holy Spirit. As you read these chapters in Acts, what do you notice about the work of the Spirit in and through these first Christians?

DAILY READINGS

> But you will receive power when the Holy Spirit comes
> upon you. And you will be my witnesses, telling people
> about me everywhere—in Jerusalem, throughout Judea,
> in Samaria, and to the ends of the earth. (Acts 1:8)

Just as Jesus had promised, the Holy Spirit was poured out on the
disciples on the day of Pentecost. They were transformed from a
frightened bunch of men and women to bold and courageous witnesses. As we read the Acts of the Apostles, we see that same Holy
Spirit continuing to fill people's lives, sometimes for the first time,
sometimes filling them afresh. The first few days this week draw your
attention to particular passages that you will have read or will be
reading as part of your Chunk Reading. As you read them, remember
that the Holy Spirit still comes to people in the same way today.

Day 1

Read **Acts 4:23-31**. As the first Christians gather together for prayer
following the arrest of Peter and John, they are filled afresh with the
Holy Spirit and go out boldly to speak of Jesus. Notice how they
begin their prayer by praising God for who he is and asserting his
greatness in the face of the threats against them. What do they ask
God for? How can our prayers be equally trusting and bold?

Day 2

In accordance with the words of Jesus in Acts 1:8, the gospel has spread into the area of Samaria through the preaching of Philip and there is 'great joy in that city' (Acts 8:8). On this occasion the new believers receive the Holy Spirit through the laying on of hands. Read **Acts 8:4-8** and **14-17**. Luke doesn't go into detail, but how do you think that Philip, Peter and John were able to tell that 'the Holy Spirit had not yet come upon any of them' (v. 16)? Luke tells us that when they laid hands on the believers they received the Holy Spirit (v. 17) but doesn't tell us what happened. What do you think might have happened so that everyone knew the Holy Spirit had been given?

Day 3

In **Acts 9:1-19** we read of the dramatic encounter between Saul and Jesus on the Damascus Road. We don't know anything else about Ananias—he was probably just an ordinary person like any of us—but he played an important part in the story (vv. 10-18). Imagine how he must have felt when he heard God asking him to go and see Saul. Are there things we can learn from this story?

Day 4

In Acts 10, Peter goes to visit Cornelius as the result of a vision that challenges his preconceptions. Read **Acts 10:34-48.** God takes the initiative and takes Peter by surprise. On this occasion, unlike in Samaria, the Holy Spirit was poured out on those who were listening while Peter was still preaching. They had not had the opportunity to respond to Peter's message, repent and be baptised. Sometimes God intervenes powerfully in people's lives when they are not expecting it. We must be careful not to try to programme the way in which God will work in our lives or those of other people. Has God ever taken you by surprise? Have you been 'taken by surprise' at all in this course?

Day 5

When the Holy Spirit came upon the disciples at Pentecost, he created a new kind of community, the Christian church. At that stage they would have seen themselves simply as Jews who believed that Jesus was the Messiah, who had been crucified and raised from the dead. That is why they continued to behave as Jews by going to worship in the Temple. This new community is beautifully described in **Acts 2:41-47**. What were its distinctive features?

Day 6

In **Acts 13:1-5**, which you will read in the next Chunk Reading, the Holy Spirit sends Paul and Barnabas to do missionary work in Cyprus and beyond. What were the five men doing when the Spirit spoke to them? How might this way of doing things fit in the church today?

Day 7

In Romans 8, Paul teaches about the work of the Spirit in the life of a Christian. Read **Romans 8:14-17** and **26-27.** What do these verses tell us about the work of the Holy Spirit in our lives?

Pray for the next group meeting that everyone will grow in their understanding of the work of the Holy Spirit.

Journal Pages

Jesus said: 'The Holy Spirit ... will
teach you everything and will remind
you of everything I have told you. I am
leaving you with a gift — peace of mind
and heart. And the peace I give is a gift
the world cannot give'.

(John 14:26-27)

Journal Pages

On the last day, the climax of the festival,
Jesus stood and shouted to the crowds,
'Anyone who is thirsty may come to me!
Anyone who believes in me may come
and drink! For the Scriptures declare,
"Rivers of living water will flow from his
heart."' (When he said 'living water,'
he was speaking of the Spirit, who would
be given to everyone believing in him. But
the Spirit had not yet been given, because
Jesus had not yet entered into his glory.)

(John 7:37-39)

Journal Pages

O thou who camest from above
the fire celestial to impart,
kindle a flame of sacred love
on the mean altar of my heart!

There let it for thy glory burn
with inextinguishable blaze,
and trembling to its source return
in humble prayer and fervent praise.

Jesus, confirm my heart's desire
to work, and speak, and think for thee;
still let me guard the holy fire,
and still stir up the gift in me.

Ready for all thy perfect will,
my acts of faith and love repeat;
till death thy endless mercies seal,
and make the sacrifice complete.

(Charles Wesley 1707–1788)

HARVEST TIME: FRUIT AND GIFTS

———

The Fruit of the Spirit

Last week we began to think about the changes brought about in our lives by the Holy Spirit. This week we begin by thinking about what Paul calls the fruit of the Holy Spirit, which you can read about in Galatians 5:19-26.

Paul contrasts what happens when people follow 'the desires of our sinful nature' with the fruit that the Holy Spirit produces in our lives. God wants us to become more and more like his Son, Jesus (Romans 8:29). The fruit of the Spirit is the character of Jesus being produced in his people. This doesn't make us clones of Jesus but rather allows his character to be formed within the unique personality God has given each one of us.

Think about fruit:

o Fruit is the natural product of a healthy tree. Effort is
   not required on the part of the tree to produce fruit!
   Our characters will become more like Jesus by our
   remaining in him, not by strenuous self-improvement
   techniques (John 15:4-5). Part of remaining in him is
   about being honest with him about our failings and
   the way we want to change. But the power to change
   comes from the Holy Spirit working in us. Change
   comes about as a result of God's grace working in us
   at our request.

o Fruit is more often seen by the onlooker: others are
   often far more aware of the changes in us than we are
   in ourselves. Perhaps you have already had comments
   from friends or family about how you are changing
   since coming on this course or being linked with the
   church.

The Gifts of the Spirit

In the last session and in our Chunk Reading we noted the important
place of signs and wonders in the life of the early church. Many of
the stories in Acts are dramatic, but the gifts of the Spirit are not
necessarily dramatic. They are simply the tool kit God has given us as
we go about his business in the world.

In 1 Corinthians 12:4-11 we have a list of nine of the gifts of
the Spirit. This is not comprehensive. There are other lists of gifts
in Romans 12 and Ephesians 4 as well as other individual gifts

mentioned throughout the New Testament. It is important that in each of the places where Paul lists gifts of the Spirit, it is in the context of teaching about the church as the body of Christ. The gifts are given to individuals as part of the church.

From 1 Corinthians 12:4-7 we can note:

- There are different kinds of gifts and of service and different ways in which God uses individuals—different people need different tools for different jobs.
- The gifts all come from the same source, God working through his Holy Spirit.
- The gifts are given so that we can help one another. **They are not trophies or toys but tools**, which are meant to be used to do something constructive for the benefit of others.

In the session, you will have looked briefly at each of the gifts listed in 1 Corinthians 12 in turn. Perhaps you have had the experience of being in the right place at the right time and saying just the right thing, which has really helped someone else. You may be unaware that you have been exercising gifts of wisdom and knowledge. This is surprisingly common. Although there may be times when we experience a dramatic healing or powerful prophecy, most of the time the gifts are the tool kit of the jobbing Christian getting on with daily life.

You can read the script of the video about the gifts of the Spirit on page 165 of this Journal.

Preparing to Receive

God does not want us simply to talk about new life in Jesus and the fruit and gifts of the Spirit. He wants us to know these things for ourselves. In Acts 2:37, which we looked at last session, the crowd asked Peter and the others, 'What should we do?' Peter replied, 'Each of you must repent of your sins and turn to God, and be baptised in the name of Jesus Christ for the forgiveness or your sins. Then you will receive the gift of the Holy Spirit. This promise is to you, to your children and to those far away' (vv. 38-39). In other words, this is for everyone.

Peter was talking about repentance and faith or trust in God. We shall look briefly at each in turn.

Repentance

Repentance is 'a change of direction':

- A conscious turning away from things that spoil our relationship with God.
- A turning towards God.

What we are turning away from is our self-centredness, which puts 'I' at the centre of our lives. This is what the Bible calls sin. But the Bible also talks about specific sins. We have read a list of specific sins already in Galatians 5:19-21. Notice the scope of this list; it includes everything from sorcery and sexual immorality to jealousy and outbursts of anger. These are not the only sins. Other lists in the

New Testament are different but similarly wide ranging. As Jesus said when he talked about taking the speck out of another's eye while not noticing the plank in our own, it is often easier to notice the faults of others than to admit our own (Matthew 7:4-5). Repentance is a decision we make, not simply a response to a feeling of guilt.

It is important if we want to make a new start with God, whether for the first time or for the thousandth time, to examine ourselves and ask the Holy Spirit to show us whether there is anything in particular that is spoiling our relationship with God. There are certain things such as occult practices which some people may have engaged in, given their prevalence in our society, that are specifically forbidden in Scripture and can cause lasting spiritual damage if not specifically confessed and renounced. Other people may be aware of certain practices that seem to have such an unshakable grip on their lives that they have become addictions. If you are aware of things that fall into either of these categories, or other things from the past that weigh heavily upon you, mention them to one of your leaders.

Faith or Trust

We exercise faith every day of our lives. For example, we sit on a chair and expect it to hold us, follow our sat nav and expect it to get us to our destination, believe the 'expert' we hear on the television or trust a friend to do what they have promised. Some things in which we put our faith or trust are more reliable than others!

On the day of Pentecost, Peter invited people to be baptised as a sign of putting their trust in Jesus Christ as Lord and Saviour. In other words, accepting all that Jesus had done for them through his death and resurrection. Faith is trusting in God and relying on him and accepting that his promises of love, forgiveness and new life are true for us personally. Faith, like repentance, is a decision we make to trust in God rather than in ourselves or anything else. It is a decision to put God at the centre of our lives.

In the Anglican Church, these promises are often used at baptism:

I repent of my sins … I renounce evil … I turn to Christ.

Peter said that if people repented and believed, then:

o   Their sins would be forgiven.
o   They would receive God's gift, the Holy Spirit.

The people believed what he had said and repented and trusted in God. Our Christian lives do not depend on our feelings at any particular time but on the character and promises of God. Of the 3,000 who were baptised at Pentecost, some would have felt deeply moved, some would have been convinced by Peter's words and some would have just felt this was the right thing to do. For all of them it was a decision they made that changed their lives.

Next Week

At next week's session there will be an opportunity to respond to what we have heard over the last few weeks.

After a short time of teaching, everyone who wishes can dedicate their lives to God through Jesus Christ and receive the laying on of hands with prayer to be filled with the Holy Spirit. Those who are already Christians and who know the fullness of the Spirit will have the opportunity to rededicate their lives, be filled afresh with the Holy Spirit and pray for their ministry within the body of Christ. Your group leaders will have explained to you whether this session will happen in your normal meeting place or elsewhere.

Thinking Back over This Session

If you would like to, jot down here any thoughts or questions you have about this week's session:

CHUNK READING

Read **Acts chapters 13-16**. Chapters 13 and 14 tell of Paul's first missionary journey. In chapter 15 we read of a major disagreement between the Jewish Christians and Paul and his friends from Antioch about whether Gentile Christians had to obey Jewish religious laws. The details of the argument may be hard for us to understand, but a very important principle was at stake—the basis on which people become Christians (15:9-11). There is nothing necessarily wrong in Christians disagreeing with one another, providing both sides are prepared for God to teach them something new and bring truth out of their discussions in the way that he did in Acts 15.

In Acts 16 we read about how the gospel first came to Europe. It is at this point that Luke joins Paul's companions and we first have passages where he says 'us' and 'we' (Acts 16:10). You might find it helpful to look up a map of Paul's missionary journeys on the internet so you can follow where he goes while reading these chapters.

Although Paul and Barnabas went their separate ways after disagreeing about whether to take Mark with them (Acts 15:36-47), at some point Paul and Mark must have been reconciled. In 2 Timothy 4:11, where Paul is in prison with only Luke as a companion, he asks Timothy to bring Mark with him when he visits as Mark 'will be helpful to me in my ministry'. Paul sets us an example here that even deep disagreements can be overcome. Barnabas is known as 'the encourager' and it is just possible that he had something to do with bringing them back together.

DAILY READINGS

> God works in different ways, but it is the same God who does the work in all of us. A spiritual gift is given to each of us so we can help each other. (1 Corinthians 12:6-7)

Day 1

Paul often contrasts the character of unbridled human nature with life in the Spirit. One place where he does that is **Galatians 5:16-26,** which we looked at in the last session. Read it again. Are there any of the 'desires of human nature' that Paul lists that are a particular temptation or failure of yours? Are there any 'fruits of the Spirit' that you would like to see more of in your life? (Remember that these are representative lists not comprehensive ones. It may be that the Holy Spirit will highlight other traits in you that God wants to transform or fruits he wishes to grow.)

Day 2

In the last session we thought about the gifts of the Spirit mentioned by Paul in 1 Corinthians 12 and how they are rather like the Christian's tool kit. Read **1 Peter 4:10-11** and notice how, rather than being specific, Peter groups them in two categories of speaking and serving. Peter, just like Paul, says that every Christian is given gifts. What can be learnt from this passage about why they are given and how they can be used?

Day 3

The story of Zacchaeus in **Luke 19:1-10**, which we read in week 1, gives us a practical example of what it means to come to Christ and repent (say sorry and change direction). In the next session you will have the opportunity to commit your life to Christ and pray to be filled with the Holy Spirit. As part of that, you will have the opportunity to make or renew these promises:

I repent of my sins.

I renounce evil.

I turn to Christ.

How ready are you to make those promises?

Day 4

To have faith is to put our trust not in our ability to help ourselves but in what Jesus has done for us by his death and resurrection. The familiar verses in **John 3:16-17** remind us that it is out of love that God has done everything necessary for us to have eternal life. Paul says the same thing in **Ephesians 2:4-10**.

If you believe in Jesus, why not rewrite John 3:16, putting your own name in place of the word 'everyone'? And then thank God for the gift of eternal life in Jesus.

Day 5

The most common thing that stops us from moving forward with Christ is fear. Some people are afraid of what other people will think of them. Others are afraid of really letting God take control of their lives. Still others are afraid that their sins and weaknesses are so great that God cannot possibly help them. Read **2 Timothy 1:7** and note the positive qualities that the Holy Spirit gives us.

Day 6

In **Luke 11:9-13**, Jesus assures his disciples that the Holy Spirit is a good gift that will be given to all who ask. What reason does Jesus give for this assurance?

Day 7

In **John 7:37-39**, Jesus gives a promise to all who are thirsty. He describes the Holy Spirit as 'rivers of living water'. What do we have to do in order to experience the Holy Spirit in this way?

Pray for the next session that everyone who asks will be filled to overflowing with the love and power of God the Holy Spirit.

Journal Pages

---

*Do not be afraid to throw
yourself on the Lord!
He will not draw back and
let you fall!
Put your worries aside and
throw yourself on him;
He will welcome you and
heal you.*

St Augustine (354-430)

Journal Pages

Just as I am, without one plea
but that you died to set me free,
and at your bidding 'Come to me!'
O Lamb of God, I come.

Just as I am, though tossed about
with many a conflict, many a doubt,
fightings within and fears without,
O Lamb of God, I come.

Just as I am, poor, wretched, blind!
Sight, riches, healing of the mind
all that I need, in you to find:
O Lamb of God, I come.

Just as I am! You will receive,
will welcome, pardon, cleanse,
    relieve:
because your promise I believe,
O Lamb of God, I come.

Just as I am! Your love unknown
has broken every barrier down:
now to be yours, yes, yours alone,
O Lamb of God, I come.

Just as I am! Of that free love
the breadth, length, depth and
    height to prove,
here for a time and then above,
O Lamb of God, I come.

Charlotte Elliott (1789-1871)

Journal Pages

Take, Lord, and receive all
my liberty, my memory, my
understanding, and all my will, all
that I have and possess. You have
given them to me; to you, O Lord, I
restore them; all things are yours,
dispose of them according to your
will. Give me your love and your
grace, for this is enough for me.

Ignatius Loyola (1491-1556)

SESSION 6

TIME FOR MINISTRY

———

Summary of Session

This week's session is different because each person will be offered the opportunity to receive prayer with the laying on of hands for the infilling of the Holy Spirit. The Journal notes are therefore very brief, but you may like to record what the session was like for you. It is amazing how quickly we can forget!

Luke 11:1-13

This passage and the next one give 'instructions' on receiving the Holy Spirit.

- The disciples had a desire for a deeper experience of God (v. 1).
- There is a need for persistence and seriousness of purpose in asking for the Spirit as in all prayer. This parable is not about God's reluctance to give (vv. 5-8)!

- The promise is sure—those who ask will receive (vv. 9-10). The Spirit is received by faith not feelings.
- God never gives us dangerous or inappropriate gifts (vv. 11-12). Therefore we should not fear any gift from our heavenly Father. (The parallel passage in Matthew 7:11 talks about 'good gifts'.)
- We must ask for the Spirit to be given to us (v. 13). Being filled with the Spirit rarely happens spontaneously.

John 7:37-39

- Verse 37 speaks of three stages: **thirsting, coming and drinking**. Think of asking for a glass of water because you are thirsty. It is no good asking for it if you don't then take it and drink from it!
- Verse 38 shows that streams go out from the Spirit-filled person into the world. We are not given the Spirit solely for ourselves. We are to be a spiritual oasis in the desert.

Use this space to record what the time of ministry was like for you.

CHUNK READING

Read **Acts chapters 17-22**. In these chapters we read how Paul and his companions preached about Jesus throughout Greece before going to Ephesus and eventually visiting Jerusalem before returning to Antioch. From there he set out on his third missionary journey, returning and strengthening the believers in Asia, Macedonia and Greece. Having met with the elders from Ephesus at Miletus, he set sail for Jerusalem knowing that trouble would await him there, as indeed it did. Once again it would be helpful to refer to a map of Paul's journeys as you read these chapters. Notice how he adapts his message to his context without losing the heart of it, which is the death and resurrection of Jesus. For instance in Athens he notices that they have an altar to 'an Unknown God' (Acts 17:22-23) and uses this to tell them about God. In these chapters, Paul faces increasing opposition. What do you think motivates him and keeps him going?

DAILY READINGS

> Anyone who belongs to Christ has become a new person. The old life is gone; a new life has begun! (2 Corinthians 5:17)

Day 1

Read **Titus 3:4-7**. This passage reminds us of the heart of the Christian good news. God's gift of new life through Jesus in the power of the Holy Spirit is for all who truly turn to him. Some people have wonderful spiritual experiences when they surrender their lives to God. Other people do not experience very much at all. Scripture reminds us that God's character and what he has done for us in Jesus are the basis of our faith and not any feelings we might or might not have. Whether or not you felt God in a special way at the last group meeting, praise him for his free gift of new life in Christ.

Pray for all who received prayer at the last group meeting, that they may know that God is with them at all times. If you did not receive prayer yourself, it may be appropriate later. If you would like to receive prayer or have questions about what happened at the last session, you don't need to wait until next week to talk it through with your group leader. The leader will be pleased to hear from you at any time this week.

Day 2

Psalm 145 in the Old Testament is a lengthy song of praise for who God is and what he has done. Read **Psalm 145:1-13**. In v. 13 the psalmist says, '[God] always keeps his promises.' If you have committed or recommitted your life to Christ, he promises, 'I will never fail you. I will never abandon you' (Hebrews 13:5). What other verses in Psalm 145 strike you as important?

Perhaps you would like to try writing your own song of praise to God. (It doesn't have to rhyme or have verses!) Or you might like to draw a picture expressing your praise. You could use the Journal pages for this.

Day 3

In Ephesians 1, Paul praises God for all the blessings we have received in Christ. Read **Ephesians 1:3-8 and 13-14** and note all the things Paul says that God has done for us. Perhaps you would like to list them here.

Now praise him for what he has done and pray that the truth of these verses may become increasingly part of your Christian experience.

Day 4

In **Ephesians 1:15-23**, Paul prays for his readers that they may grow. Why not pray verses 17-20 for yourself and other members of your group?

Day 5

Proverbs 3:5-8 in the Old Testament gives some wise advice for those who wish to follow God's plan for their lives. Does any part of this strike you as particularly important?

Day 6

When the Spirit of truth is invited into our lives, one of the things he often does is to show up the dark places that need forgiveness and cleansing. Read **1 John 1:5-2:2,** towards the end of the New Testament. These verses remind us what to do when we become aware of sin in our lives. It might be helpful to write down the promises God gives us in 1:9 and 2:2.

Day 7

If you have been doing the Chunk Reading from Acts, you will realise that being a Christian is no guarantee of an easy life. **James 1:2-8** says we ought to think ourselves fortunate when problems arise because they give us the opportunity to strengthen our faith. Are there any difficulties that you have met recently that have both challenged and strengthened your faith?

Pray for your next group meeting as members will have the opportunity to share the experiences of the past week.

Journal Pages

All praise to God, the Father of our
Lord Jesus Christ, who has blessed
us with every spiritual blessing in
the heavenly realms because we are
united with Christ.

(Ephesians 1:3)

Journal Pages

Glory to the Father and to the Son
and to the Holy Spirit
as it was in the beginning is now
and shall be for ever.

Journal Pages

Praise, my soul, the King of heaven;
to his feet your tribute bring.
Ransomed, healed, restored, forgiven,
who like me his praise should sing.
Alleluia, alleluia!
Praise the everlasting King!

Praise him for his grace and favour
to his people in distress.
Praise him, still the same as ever,
slow to chide, and swift to bless.
Alleluia, alleluia!
Glorious in his faithfulness!

Father-like he tends and spares us;
well our feeble frame he knows.
In his hand he gently bears us,
rescues us from all our foes.
Alleluia, alleluia!
Widely as his mercy flows!

Angels, help us to adore him;
you behold him face to face.
Sun and moon, bow down before him,
dwellers all in time and space.
Alleluia, alleluia!
Praise with us the God of grace!

(Henry Francis Lyte 1793-1847)

SESSION 7

GROWING UP

_____

Facts and Feelings

1 John 5:13 reminds us that God wants us to be confident that we are Christians.

Feelings may come and go but our faith is founded on fact:

- The fact of Christ's incarnation, death and resurrection
- The promises of God found in Scripture
- The fact of our profession of faith (made either in the ministry time last week or on another occasion)

The public profession of faith at baptism/confirmation/being received into fellowship reinforces these facts and makes them more objective.

Jesus promises not only to welcome and receive us if we come to him, but to stay with us. He reassures us that we have new life in him:

- o 'Those the Father has given me will come to me, and I will never reject them' (John 6:37).
- o 'I am with you always' (Matthew 28:20).
- o 'Look! I stand at the door and knock. If you hear my voice and open the door, I will come in, and we will share a meal together as friends' (Revelation 3:20).
- o 'Anyone who belongs to Christ has become a new person. The old life is gone; a new life has begun!' (2 Corinthians 5:17).
- o 'God has said, "I will never fail you. I will never abandon you." So we can say with confidence, "The LORD is my helper, so I will have no fear. What can mere people do to me?"' (Hebrews 13:5b-6).

Afterwards—Difficulties and Opportunities

What happens once we have become a Christian or been freshly filled with the Holy Spirit?

After his baptism, 'Jesus, full of the Holy Spirit ... was led by the Spirit in the wilderness, where he was tempted by the devil for forty days' (Luke 4:1-2).

Whenever we take a significant move forward in our relationship with God, there will be both difficulties and opportunities.

Difficulties may include:

- o **Being misunderstood**—by family or friends.
- o **Having doubts**—we all do from time to time. Remember the disciples after the resurrection?

- **Feeling guilty**—as our consciences become more sensitive to sin or the Holy Spirit brings to the surface things from the past that need dealing with. Remember that God is always ready to forgive (1 John 1:9) and that there is no condemnation for those who belong to Christ Jesus (Romans 8:1).
- **Experiencing challenges**—life doesn't always run smoothly and becoming a Christian does not assure us of an easy passage—on the contrary! But we are given a new strength to deal with difficulties and they can be used constructively (James 1:2-5).

If we ask God to use us then **'Opportunities'** may include:

- **Sharing our faith**—as people ask questions or notice how we are changing
- **Helping others**—demonstrating God's love in practical ways
- **Praying for others**—and seeing God answer prayer
- **Seeing God work through us**—as we begin to grow in the gifts of the Spirit

Growing as a Christian

In John 15:1-10, Jesus gives us a picture of himself as the vine and ourselves as the branches. We are intended to grow and be fruitful, but if this is to happen we need to stay close to Jesus. Broken branches soon wither.

Healthy plants need a variety of nutrients, the right conditions for growth and a gardener looking after them. God is the gardener, but he also uses other members of the church, especially leaders, to help us to grow.

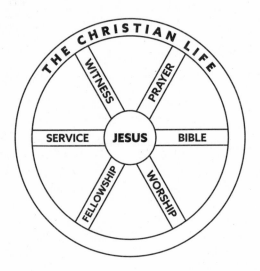

God has provided various means by which we can receive his goodness and grow closer to him. If it is to run smoothly then all the 'spokes' are of equal importance.

- **Prayer**—both personal daily prayer in the way we have encouraged through the Journal and joining with others for prayer.
- **Bible**—both reading the Bible regularly for ourselves, possibly with the aid of Bible reading notes or an app, and joining in Bible study with others.

- o **Worship**—meeting regularly with other Christians for worship, prayer and teaching. Jesus commanded us to share bread and wine as he did with his first disciples. The Lord's Supper or Holy Communion is one very important way of meeting with Jesus and being fed and strengthened by him. He also told his followers that new disciples should be baptised.
- o **Fellowship**—meeting with other Christians to encourage one another in the faith. This is different from simply having a coffee and chat after a service.
- o **Service**—we have been filled with the Holy Spirit so that we can work with Jesus for the coming of his kingdom. We have been equipped with the gifts of the Spirit as tools. Some service is best done alongside other people.
- o **Witness**—praying for courage and taking the opportunities God gives us to share our faith.

Thinking Back over This Session

If you would like to, jot down here any thoughts or questions you have about this week's session:

BIBLE READING AND PRAYER

Your leaders may have suggested various resources that they have found helpful. There are, of course, numerous Bible study resources on the internet. If you want to know more about a particular passage, simply type the reference into a search engine and you will be able to see commentaries and even sermons on it. As with anything on the internet, you need to look at several links and will find some more helpful or reliable than others.

Here are a few websites and apps that you may find helpful:

- **www.biblesociety.org.uk** has lots of useful introductory articles about the Bible.
- **www.bible.com** and the YouVersion app, which you may already be using, have lots of Bible reading plans on different themes.
- **www.brf.org.uk** has information about different series of daily Bible reading aids that you can buy, and useful sections on prayer and discipleship.
- **www.bibleinoneyear.org** has a free Bible reading app with an audio commentary by Nicky and Pippa Gumbel.
- Some denominations produce their own apps for daily prayer and Bible reading. The Church of England app is called 'Daily Prayer' and there are daily notes in 'Reflections for Daily Prayer' based on the lectionary readings for each day. You can also access these at

www.churchofengland.org. The Methodist Church has a daily Bible study called 'A Word in Time' and a 'Prayer of the Day' at www.methodist.org.uk.

o www.preachweb.org/biblemonth offers thirty days focused on a single book of the Bible for churches, groups and individuals.

o www.sacredspace.ie and www.pray-as-you-go.org are two Jesuit sites which many people who are not Roman Catholic also find helpful.

o www.24-7prayer.com has a variety of prayer apps and other resources.

Why not jot down here details of websites the leaders have recommended or that you have discovered that have been helpful?

CHUNK READING

This week the story of the early church as recorded in Acts reaches its climax as Paul finally reaches Rome, at that time the centre of the known world. Read **chapters 23-28,** which tell of Paul's courage as he faces both legal trials and physical danger, confident that God's ultimate purposes cannot be thwarted by human beings. We don't know what happened to him once he reached Rome, but several of his letters recorded in the New Testament were probably written from there.

As you reflect back over your Chunk Reading of Acts, what things strike you as important to remember?

DAILY READINGS

> I am the vine; you are the branches. Those who remain in me, and I in them, will produce much fruit. For apart from me you can do nothing. (John 15:5)

Day 1

If we are to grow as Christians then there needs to be a degree of determination and persistence. Read **Colossians 2:6-7** and note what Paul says we should do to become mature Christians.

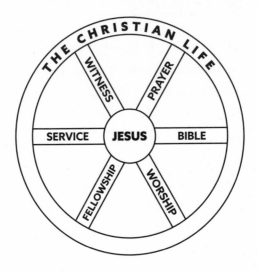

The six things on the spokes of the wheel mentioned in the last session are means that God has provided to help us keep our roots deep in Christ and our lives securely built upon him. Are there any that you need to develop or add as a regular part of your life?

Day 2

In **Luke 6:46-49**, Jesus tells a story about the importance of laying strong foundations for our lives. How does he say this should be done? What do you think he means? What might be the strong foundations of your life?

Day 3

Ephesians 6:10-18 describes the Christian life as a spiritual battle against the forces of evil. These were defeated at the cross but are still active in the world until Jesus returns and his kingdom comes in its fullness. Make a list of the armour that God has provided for us.

It can be very helpful to consciously put on the armour of God, especially when we are being tempted or facing particular troubles or difficulties. Note that every bit of the armour is something that Christ has already given us. All we are asked to do is put it on and stand firm.

Day 4

One of the spokes in the wheel is reading and studying the Bible. In **2 Timothy 3:14-17**, Paul reminds his younger colleague why studying the Scriptures is so important. What does he say that the Scriptures are useful for? Have you found them helpful in any of these ways?

During Saints Alive! you have been introduced to ways of studying the Bible together, chunk reading and the daily reading of short passages. There are other ways that many people find helpful. In these days of easy internet access, we are blessed with many more resources to help us than Christians in the past. In **1 Peter 2:2** we are encouraged to feed on God, and one way of doing this is through the Scriptures. 'Like newborn babies, you must crave pure spiritual milk so that you will grow into a full experience of salvation.'

Day 5

Another way in which we can feed spiritually is by coming regularly to Holy Communion, sometimes called the Eucharist/Mass/Lord's Supper. In **John 6:47-58** we read how Jesus speaks of himself as 'the bread of life'. When we share the bread and wine in Holy Communion, we are reminded how Jesus was broken for us on the cross so that we might know eternal life. This is a present reality as well as a promise for the future.

Day 6

Where the other gospels record the story of the Last Supper, John adds something else which happened that evening that he thought was important. Read **John 13:1-17** where Jesus washes his disciples feet and sets them an example of how they should relate to one another. When we serve other people, whether they are Christians or not, we are following the example of Jesus. Are there ways in which you already serve others? Do you think that as the course ends God might be calling you to other forms of service?

Day 7

Read **1 Peter 2:4-10**. Here Peter talks about the church being made up of 'living stones' with Christ as the cornerstone that holds the whole building together. The purpose of the church, he says, is to be both a company of worshippers and a place where other people can encounter and worship God. He recognises that not everyone will want to share our faith. For some people Jesus is a 'stone that makes people stumble' (v. 8). However, our responsibility is to 'show others the goodness of God' (v. 9) as those who have experienced for ourselves God's love and mercy.

Thank God for the members of your group and all that you have learnt from one another. Pray for your meeting today as you talk together about what it means to be the church.

Journal Pages

———

Open my eyes that I may see,
incline my heart that I may desire
order my steps that I may follow
the way of your commandments.

Lancelot Andrews (1555-1626)

Journal Pages

May God give you more and more grace and peace as you grow in your knowledge of God and Jesus our Lord.

(2 Peter 1:2)

Journal Pages

Do not be afraid, for I have
ransomed you. I have called you
by name; you are mine. When you
go through deep waters, I will be
with you. When you go through
rivers of difficulty, you will not
drown.... You are precious to me.
You are honoured, and I love you.

(Isaiah 43:1–2, 4)

SESSION 8

BEING CHURCH

———

The Body of Christ

When we become Christians, we become part of a body—one of the images used in the New Testament to describe the church. It was the picture used by Paul in 1 Corinthians 12 when we were thinking about the gifts of the Spirit. In this session we are going to look at a similar passage in Romans.

In Romans 12:4-5, Paul tells us that:

- There are many different parts to a body but they all belong (v. 4).
- Each part has its own job to do.
- There is an essential unity in Christ (v. 5) that all Christians share. We may not always like our fellow Christians and would not necessarily choose them as friends, but they are family, and as family we are called to love one another. This love applies not only

to those in our local fellowship but to Christians around the world, including those who are very different from ourselves and especially those who are suffering for their faith.

In verses 6-8, Paul uses a number of specific gifts as illustrations: prophecy, service, teaching, etc.

- Each Christian is called to make some specific contribution to the life of the community and to do so to the best of their ability. This contribution is called their 'ministry', the work for which God has particularly gifted and called us.
- We shall not necessarily discover this ministry immediately.
- Other Christians may be able to help us by telling us how they see God's gifts emerging in our lives.

In many secondary schools, pupils begin by taking all the subjects in the curriculum. As they progress up the school, they take fewer and fewer subjects at greater depth. Eventually, whether they go on to further education or employment, they may end up specialising in one particular area. As they progress, they will benefit from guidance from their teachers to find the right subjects to take. For most people something similar happens within the context of the church. When we are new Christians, we need to explore which gifts God might be giving us and how they might be used in our particular church. After a while we may find ourselves being used regularly in particular ways. This could well be an indication of the way in which God has gifted us.

- o Whatever we are called to do, we should tackle it with determination and enthusiasm (v. 11).
- o Notice again the importance of love and respect for our fellow Christians (vv. 9-10). Remember that love can be very practical (v. 13).

Guidance

The question of 'How do I know what God wants me to do?' arises not just when it comes to discovering our gifts and ministries. It is an important question for the whole of our lives, e.g., work, marriage, family decisions. It is too big a topic to cover in detail in this course, but the beginning of Romans 12 is a good place to start.

In Romans 12:1-2, notice the final sentence, 'Then you will learn to know God's will for you.' In order to find God's will, we must first:

- o Dedicate our lives to him (v. 1).
- o Stop thinking in the world's way, i.e., 'Don't copy the behaviour and customs of this world' (v. 2). (One translator says graphically, 'Don't let the world around you squeeze you into its own mould' [PHILLIPS].)

○ Let God transform our thinking (v. 2). This happens as we study Scripture, pray, listen to Christian teaching and talk with one another.

In the Greek these verses are in the plural. God's will is often to be found in talking and praying with others and not in lonely struggling as an individual.

The Church Member

As Saints Alive! draws to a close, you will have had an opportunity in your group meeting of talking very practically about what it means to be a member of your particular church. Churches are wonderfully varied. Some are more traditional and some more experimental. Whatever your church is like, if you are to go on growing as a Christian, it is important that you belong to it.

Your group leaders may have adapted what follows to fit your particular church. If so you are welcome to stick their sheet on top of this or to put yours alongside. They may invite you to take their sheet away and sign it as part of your commitment to follow Jesus in the context of your local church.

I, _____,
have decided before Christ that I will seek his help to be a loyal
member of _____ Church.
As a loyal member I will:

- Be regular in worship and prepare for it with care.
- Join with others in fellowship, prayer and study.
- Give care and practical help to others, both members of the church and those outside, especially to those in the greatest need.
- Give regular financial support to the church.
- Seek to discover and exercise the gifts God has given to me.
- Pray for other members of the church and especially for those in leadership.
- Accept and support the leadership—not unthinkingly but as a responsible adult.
- Avoid gossiping about or criticising others. Talking to people directly and not behind their backs.
- Continue to think about my faith and how it relates to my home, work, recreation and other parts of my life.
- Seek to share my faith with others by praying for them, looking for opportunities to speak to them and inviting them to church events or groups.

Signed_____ Date _____

This is a model commitment. All of us will find ourselves falling short on occasion. When this happens, recognise it, say sorry and carry on!

After the Course

Finally, in this session your group leaders will help you to explore opportunities to continue to grow in faith and to build upon what you have received together as a group. You will be invited to share your hopes and expectations as the course comes to an end. You might like to note them here along with anything else you particularly want to remember from this session.

CHUNK READING

Last week we completed our reading of Acts and left Paul imprisoned in Rome. Although he was in prison, his ministry didn't stop. His imprisonment probably took the form of house arrest. He may have been chained to his guards but his friends would be free to visit him, bring him food and run errands on his behalf. It was when he was in prison that Paul wrote many of his letters. As you will realise from Acts, he wasn't just imprisoned in Rome.

It was when he was imprisoned, either in Rome or possibly Ephesus, that Paul wrote to the Christians at Philippi. You can find the story of his first visit and the founding of the church there in Acts 16. His letter to the Philippians is one of his shortest and probably one of the easiest to understand. It is written to encourage the Christians there as they too faced opposition and possibly persecution. Paul's evident love for them and joy in the gospel shines through this letter. So does his commitment to following Jesus whatever the cost.

Read **Philippians**. It is only four chapters long. Make a note of anything that particularly encourages you or challenges you. Don't worry too much about bits that you don't understand at this stage. You might like to come back to it later with a commentary or to study it in a small group.

DAILY READINGS

I can do everything through Christ, who gives me
strength. (Philippians 4:13)

Day 1

In the last session we thought together about what it means to be part
of the church. Read again **Romans 12:3-8**, where Paul talks about
being the body of Christ and each person having different gifts. Have
you any idea yet which gifts God might have given you? Spend some
time praying that you may be open to all the ways he wants to use
you.

Day 2

Read **Romans 12:9-21**. You looked at some of these verses in the
last session but not all of them. Paul is saying that the quality of
our life together as Christians is important. If we are the body of
Christ, then when people look at the church they should be able to
see Jesus. Some of what he says in these verses is very challenging.
Which bits do you think you might find hardest to live up to? In

your prayers don't just pray for yourself but also for other members of your church family, especially any you don't find it easy to like.

Day 3

Another place where Paul talks about the church as the body of Christ is in Ephesians 4. Read **Ephesians 4:1-10**. In this passage he emphasises how much we have in common and how important it is to try to maintain the unity of the church. He also reminds his readers that each one has been given a special gift to use for the blessing of others. Thank God for all you share in common with other Christians, not just locally but throughout the world.

Day 4

Read **Ephesians 4:11-16**. In this passage Paul doesn't list gifts of the Spirit as he did in Romans 12 or 1 Corinthians 12. Here he singles out the particular gifts or ministries that are required by church leaders whose job it is to help the whole church grow and work together properly. What are they (v. 11)? No one person can possibly have all these gifts even if many churches only have one minister, pastor or vicar. This means that other people, usually those who have not been ordained, will be called by God to positions of leadership in the local church. Do you know who these people are in your church? They need your prayers and support if they are to fulfil their callings.

Day 5

In the previous chapter of Ephesians, Paul prayed for the church in Ephesus. It was a BIG prayer. You can find it in **Ephesians 3:14-21**. Why not read it slowly several times and make it your own? Perhaps you may want to make a note of anything in it that you especially wish to remember.

Day 6

When we are a Christian, it becomes important to us to live in the way God wants. This is not just about our lifestyles and attitudes and relationships, important though these are. It also means that we will want to do what God wants in the whole of our lives. We will want to include God in the big decisions we make. It is not always easy to discern what is right but, as we thought together in the last session, a good place to begin is with **Romans 12:1-2**. It's a sort of step-by-step recipe for finding out the will of God. You can jot down the four steps that lead up to 'then you will learn to know God's will for you'.

Day 7

This week the Chunk Reading has been from Paul's letter to the **Philippians**. Perhaps a good place to finish these daily readings is with the instructions that Paul gives to them in **4:4-9**.

However, although these daily notes have finished, please don't stop reading your Bible and praying. Above everything else, these are the things that will keep you close to God and help you to go on growing as a Christian.

Journal Pages

_____

Teach us, good Lord,
to serve you as you deserve,
to give and not to count the cost,
to fight and not to hear the
    wounds,
to toil and not to seek for rest,
to labour and not to ask for any
    reward
save that of knowing that we do
    your will.

St Ignatius Loyola (1491-1556)

Journal Pages

When I think of all this, I fall to my knees and
pray to the Father, the Creator of everything
in heaven and on earth. I pray that from his
glorious, unlimited resources he will empower
you with inner strength through his Spirit.
Then Christ will make his home in your hearts
as you trust in him. Your roots will grow
down into God's love and keep you strong.
And may you have the power to understand,
as all God's people should, how wide, how
long, how high, and how deep his love is. May
you experience the love of Christ, though it is
too great to understand fully. Then you will be
made complete with all the fullness of life and
power that comes from God.

Now all glory to God, who is able, through
his mighty power at work within us, to
accomplish infinitely more than we might ask
or think. Glory to him in the church and in
Christ Jesus through all generations forever
and ever! Amen.

(Ephesians 3:14-21)

Journal Pages

Lord, make me an instrument of your
    peace.
Where there is hatred, let me sow love;
Where there is error, truth;
Where there is injury, pardon;
Where there is doubt, faith;
Where there is despair, hope;
Where there is darkness, light;
And where there is sadness, joy.
O Divine Master, grant that I may not
    so much seek
To be consoled as to console;
To be understood as to understand;
To be loved as to love.
For it is in giving that we receive;
It is in pardoning that we are
    pardoned;
It is in self-forgetting that we find;
And it is in dying to ourselves that we
    are born to eternal life.
Amen.

(Attributed to St Francis of Assisi)

JOURNALING

———

The Saints Alive! course is coming to an end, but your journey with God may just be beginning.

Have you found adding your thoughts and reflections to the blank pages in this Journal helpful? Many people do.

Perhaps you could think about starting a journal of your own to record the next part of your journey. Why not buy yourself a new book, perhaps with a nice cover, that you can keep as something special? You might like to invest in a special pen to go with it and, if you are someone who has enjoyed sketching and colouring during the course, some coloured pencils too.

At the beginning you could write a Bible verse that really speaks to you.

If someone took a group photo at the end of Saints Alive!, why not stick that in as well and write a brief summary of what the course has meant to you?

Then start looking out for things that speak to you:

- A verse from a favourite hymn or song
- A postcard you see in a shop or a photo you take

- A sentence from a letter or text, or comment someone makes
  - A poem
    - A prayer
      - A story that touches you
        - A Bible verse
          - Anything that speaks to you about God and your Christian journey

If thoughts and ideas come to you when you are praying, reading your Bible or another book, listening to a sermon or a podcast, write them down. Make a note of any decisions or resolves you make.

Some people like to write their prayers when they are praying about something important. Other people like to use their journals to keep a note of people or situations they are praying for.

You don't have to write or draw every day, just when there is something you want to remember or think about further. Don't feel guilty about leaving it for a bit. Get into a rhythm that suits you.

Just like your Saints Alive! Journal, it's yours to use as you like!

Journal Pages

Journal Pages

Journal Pages

Journal Pages

Journal Pages

Journal Pages

Journal Pages

Journal Pages

APPENDIX

―――

Video Scripts

In this part of the Journal you will find the scripts from the teaching videos used during the course and also an article about the evidence for the resurrection.

Session 1: The Two Sons

There was a farmer who had two sons. One day, the younger son came to him and said, 'I'm going to inherit lots of this estate, but I'd like it now so that I can enjoy it while I'm young.' The father had a great love for his sons, and so he divided up his estate and gave it to them. The younger son took all of his money and set off for another country. He used the money to party away. He lived the high life. Meanwhile, the older brother was working away in the fields day after day. The father kept looking out for the younger son, hoping that he would come home, but each day he was disappointed.

The younger son spent his money, and one day he opened his purse and discovered it was all gone. He could no longer join his so-called friends and live the high life. He managed to find a job feeding pigs; it was barely enough to survive. 'What have I done?' he said to himself. 'I have been a fool. I am not worthy to be my father's son; his servants are eating better than I am. I'll go back home, I'll tell him what a fool I've been, and I'll ask him if I can have a job as one of his servants.'

The father, looking out for his son, one day sees him trudging across the fields towards him. He races towards him with excitement, with joy, and he flings his arms around him.

The son says to his father, 'Father, I'm not worthy to be called your son. I've sinned against you and against heaven.' But the father calls the servants and says, 'Bring new clothes and bring new shoes, place them on my son instead of these rags.' He took a ring and put it on his son's finger, 'This says that you are still part of my family.' Then he said to the servants, 'We are going to throw the biggest party ever to celebrate the fact that my son, who was lost, is now found. He was dead, but he's now alive.'

Meanwhile, the oldest son is out working in the fields. The party gets started and there is dancing and joy, and it's noisy. The older son comes towards the house and asks one of the servants, 'What's all this commotion?' 'Your younger brother is back,' they say, 'and we're celebrating.' The brother is furious and he refuses to come in. His father comes out and pleads with him, 'Come and celebrate with us.' But the older brother says, 'Why? This younger brother of mine, who's wasted your money, you've thrown the red carpet out for him. Whereas I, who served you every day, has never had a party.' But the father said to him, 'You have supported me every day. But your younger brother, he was lost and is now found. He was dead and is alive, and we should celebrate.'

Session 1: The Cottage

Imagine a beautiful cottage designed to be an ideal home, and yet this cottage has become derelict. The garden is overgrown. There's a hole in the roof and the floorboards are completely rotten. Someone comes along and they see this cottage. They see its potential and they buy it. They set about the work of restoration. This is no amateur. This is someone who is an expert with vast experience. They know exactly what to do to bring this cottage back to its former glory, and the order they need to do things in. They know the drastic jobs and also the less obvious jobs, and they won't stop until the cottage is completely restored and mended.

The Bible says that God bought you with a high price, and in Christ we are being renewed and restored to be just like him. God knows us as individuals and he knows the particular things that are needed to restore us, and he sets about the work with love. Some of the jobs that need doing are drastic like ripping up the rotten floorboards and others are less obvious and unknown to others, but God knows. And God also knows what we can take and how fast that change can happen. He won't go at a pace that means the structure can't hold: the cottage won't collapse. Sometimes the jobs that God is working on in us are obvious and sometimes they're not, but he's working and we don't need to fear change. Neither do we need to be dismayed when it feels like he's working on others faster than us. He won't give up on us. Jesus has come to show us God's love for us, a love that cannot be earned, and he longs for each of us to know his forgiveness and have our relationships mended.

Session 2: The Message of the Cross

This film portrays in dramatic fashion the last days of Christ's life, largely using the words of the Bible.... It is the greatest drama that has ever happened. Indeed it is the centre of history itself.

It all starts calmly enough. Jesus and his followers were on the road up to Jerusalem. Jesus took the twelve disciples aside and told them of the things that were going to happen to him. 'We are going to Jerusalem where the Son of Man will be handed over to the priests and the teachers of the law.' They will condemn him to death and hand him over to the Gentiles. They will make fun of him, spit on him, whip him, kill him—but after three days he will be raised to life. The disciples did not understand what he meant and were afraid to ask. So Jesus began to set the scene for the final act.

As they came near to Jerusalem Jesus sent two of his disciples on ahead, 'Go to the village ahead of you. As soon as you get there you will find a colt tied up that has never been ridden: untie it and bring it here.' They brought the colt, and threw their cloaks over it, and Jesus got on. Many people spread their cloaks on the road, while others cut branches from the fields trees and spread them on the road. The people began to shout, 'Praise God. God bless him who comes in the name of the Lord. Praise God!' It was a scene of wild enthusiasm. The miracle-worker from the north had come. They were giving him a reception fit for a king. But in Jerusalem Jesus was going to mount a different kind of throne than the one they expected.

Next day he went into the Temple and began to drive out all those who were buying and selling. He overturned the tables of the money-changers and the stools of those who sold pigeons. He cried out, 'The Scriptures say, "My house shall be called a house of prayer for all people," but you have made it a hideout for thieves.'

Every day Jesus taught in the Temple. The chief priests wanted to kill him but they could not find a way to do it without rousing the crowd which followed him. And so they began to draw a net of intrigue around him—a net drawn by the people who called themselves religious. Their plot led to the death of the greatest man who had ever lived. Beneath their conspiracy there was a deeper plan—the will of God. For Jesus had said, 'When I am lifted up from the earth I shall draw everyone to me.'

But how could they kill him without the people knowing? Out of the blue there came their answer. Judas Iscariot, one of the twelve disciples, went to them and offered to betray Jesus.

They promised to give him money and Judas began to look for an opportunity to betray Jesus. For the high priests, in their uncertainty and confusion as to what to do with Jesus, it must have seemed as if it had been handed to them on a plate. Here, in the middle of his band of disciples, was a traitor.

On the first day of the feast of unleavened bread, Jesus sent two of his disciples into the city to prepare for the Passover meal. 'You'll see a man carrying a water jar. Follow him and he will show where you can get a meal ready for us.' It was Thursday—what we now call Maundy Thursday—the day of the Last Supper. During the meal Jesus rose, took off his outer garments, and tied a towel round his waist. He began to wash his disciples' feet. 'You should wash one another's feet,' he told them. When he was back at the table, he said to them, 'One of you who is sharing this meal with me will betray me.' 'Is it I, Lord?' they all asked.

'It is the man to whom I will give this piece of bread.' And Judas took the bread and went out. He went out into the night—into the dark hell of his own soul.

Jesus took some bread and gave thanks to God. Then he broke it in pieces and gave it to the disciples, saying, 'This is my body, which is given for you.' Then he took a cup, gave thanks to God and handed it to them. And they all drank from it. 'This is my blood which is poured out for many. I tell you, I will never again drink this wine until I drink the new wine in the Kingdom of God.' And so he was host at this meal, which we remember and re-enact even to this day. The meal of the life of Jesus.

Jesus and the disciples then went out to the Mount of Olives. They came to a place called Gethsemane. Jesus said to his disciples, 'Sit here while I pray.' Distress and anguish came over him and he said to them, 'The sorrow in my heart is so great that it almost crushes me. Stay here and watch.' He went a little further on, threw himself on the ground ... and prayed that if possible he might not have to go through the time of suffering. 'Father, my Father, all things are possible to you. Take this cup from me—but not what I want but what you want.'

Then he returned and found the disciples asleep. 'Are you asleep? Could you not keep awake for one hour?' While he was still talking, Judas arrived. With him was a crowd armed with swords and clubs. 'Teacher,' he said, and he stepped forward and kissed Jesus. They arrested Jesus and brought him to the High Priest's house. The Jewish court had gathered and they brought many witnesses against Jesus, but they told lies and contradicted each other. Jesus was silent. The court voted against him. He was guilty of blasphemy and should be put to death. They had a problem to overcome, for they could not carry out the sentence of death: only the Romans—the occupying power—could do that.

Meanwhile, Peter was in the courtyard below. One of the servant girls who worked for the high priest came by and noticed Peter warming himself at the fire. She looked at him closely and said, 'You were one of those with Jesus of Nazareth.'

But Peter denied it. 'I don't know what you're talking about.' Just then, a rooster crowed. And so Peter denied his Lord.

They bound Jesus, led him off and handed him over to Pilate, the Roman governor. Pilate, on learning that he came from Galilee, sent him to Herod who ruled that region. Herod hoped to see Jesus perform some miracle and questioned him. But Jesus made no answer so Herod mocked him and sent him back to Pilate who examined him further. Herod is one of those people who have an interest in religious questions. He would argue all night long. He was interested in this sort of thing—but he never came to the point of decision.

Pilate called together the leading priests. He announced his verdict: 'You brought this man to me. I have examined him thoroughly and find him innocent. Nothing this man has done calls for the death penalty.'

At the Passover it was the habit of Pilate to set free a prisoner that the people asked for. 'Do you want me to release Jesus, the one who is called King of the Jews?' 'Kill him. Set Barabbas free.' Now Barabbas was a rebel and a murderer. 'Kill him. Set Barabbas free.' Pilate still wanted to set Jesus free. He appealed to the crowd again but they just shouted back, 'Crucify him, crucify him!' Then Pilate took water and washed his hands. 'I am not responsible for the death of this man. This is your doing.' As though, by just washing his hands, Pilate could clear himself of some of the guilt for the death of Jesus. He knew that Jesus was innocent. He had said so, but because of his weakness he was prepared to let Jesus be killed. And so he set Barabbas, the murderer, free.

His solders took Jesus and whipped him. They plaited a crown of thorns and placed it on his head. They put a purple robe on him as though it was the purple of the emperor and they mocked him, kneeling before him, 'Long live the King of Jews!' They spat on him, struck him.

Pilate, seeing him, said, 'Look, here is the man,' and handed him over to be crucified.

Jesus went out carrying the cross to the place of execution. But what he had suffered already was too much. He stumbled under the weight of the cross, so the soldiers seized a man called Simon from Cyrene and forced him to carry Jesus' cross.

When they came to Golgotha, the Place of the Skull, they offered Jesus wine mixed with a drug called myrrh. But he would not drink it. So they crucified him, nailing him to the cross. Through it all Jesus kept repeating, 'Father forgive them: they don't know what they're doing.'

The soldiers divided his clothes amongst themselves, throwing dice to see who would get each piece—one of the perks for doing a difficult job.

The people passing by shook their heads and threw insults, 'You were going to tear down the Temple and build it up again in three days. Now come down from the cross and save yourself.' The chief priests and the teachers of the law also jeered at him among themselves: 'He saved others, but he can't save himself. Let him come down from that cross and then we will believe in him.'

They also crucified two criminals with Jesus—one on his right and the other on his left. One mocked him, 'Save yourself—and us.' But the other said, 'Jesus, remember me when you come into your Kingdom.' Jesus said to him, 'I promise you, today you will be with me in paradise.'

Jesus saw his mother standing there with John the disciple. He said to her, 'Mother, there is your son. John, here is your mother.' Jesus did not want his mother to see his hour of deepest agony and so John led her away.

At noon the country was covered with a thick darkness which lasted for three hours. At three o'clock in the afternoon Jesus cried out, *'Eloi, Eloi, lama sabachthani'* which means, 'My God, my God, why have you abandoned me.' Jesus was bearing upon himself the guilt and the sin and the pain and the whole world. He felt let down by his Father, abandoned and alone. And then Jesus gave another loud cry, but this time it was not one of desolation: it was a cry of victory which has rung round the world, 'It is finished!' And he bowed his head and died.

At that moment the curtain hanging in the Temple, which separated the people from the Holy of Holies, was torn in two from top to bottom. The barrier which stood between us and God had split. The way was now open for all to enter into the Kingdom of God.

There was an earthquake, the graves were opened and many who had died were raised to life.

The army officer who was standing in front of the cross saw how Jesus had died, and said, 'This man truly was the Son of God.' And so he, the second person, came to faith in Christ through the cross.

Some women were there, watching from a distance. They had followed Jesus while he was in Galilee and had helped him. They were seeing the death of their dreams.

The soldiers broke the legs of the two men who were crucified with Jesus. When they came to Jesus they saw that he was already dead and did not break his legs. One of the soldiers however, pierced Jesus' side with a spear and immediately blood and water flowed out.

Pilate was approached by Joseph of Arimathea who asked for permission to take down Jesus' body. He took it into a garden and there in a new tomb laid the body of Jesus. The women who had been with Jesus went with Joseph and saw the tomb and where Jesus' body was placed in it. And Joseph rolled a large stone over the entrance to the tomb.

It seemed as though it was the end of the story:

... the wandering preacher had eventually ended up on a cross.

But it wasn't. Because Good Friday is followed by Easter Day. The stone did not remain in front of the tomb. The tomb was broken open by the power of the living God. Jesus was raised from death to life and opened for us the gateway of eternal life!

...

There are various attitudes you and I can take to the death of Christ.

We can be like the passers-by. They just gave a casual glance and then went on their way. It is the response of apathy—a topic of conversation for a few minutes and then forgotten. A snippet at the bottom of the column in the local paper. We glance at the crucifix-ion, shudder at the barbarity of it and then turn our back.

... or we can be hostile like those who jeered at Christ and flung his fate in his face. We can reject him and his claims on our life with anger and denial.

... or we can be like the army officer, saying, 'Truly this man was the Son of God.'

... or like the criminal on the cross—'Jesus remember me when you come into your Kingdom.'

The cross always asks a question. 'What do you make of Jesus?' Our answer can be, 'My Lord and my God.'

Session 3: Mary in the Garden

It was quiet now in the garden. The sun had risen, and the dew was still on the grass. You could still see the footprints of those who had been in the garden that morning. The women who had come slowly carrying their spices, and then there was confusion and uncertainty and the footprints had gone back to where they had come from. Then there were the footprints of two men who had come running, stopped, and stared and then gone away again. There had been noise and loud voices as confusion reigned, but now it was still. And there was just Mary Magdalene sobbing in the garden of the tomb where they had laid the body of Jesus after that terrible Friday. She knew that the body had gone—she had been there that morning, but where was it? Who had taken it?

Mary and Jesus went back to the time when Jesus had healed her. He had taken away from her all that had disturbed her, and from that moment she had stayed close to him. She had followed him every-where. She supported him from her wealth, and she had been there as he died, a torturous death on the cross. She had heard him say with his final breath, 'Father, into your hands, I commit my spirit.' And then she had helped as they lay the body in the tomb. But now the stone was rolled away, the guards were gone and there was nobody.

She saw two strange figures. She said to them, 'If you have taken my Lord away, tell me where he is?' But there was no answer. And then she saw another figure standing near her. The figure asked her, 'Who are you looking for?' Blinded by her tears, Mary thought this was the gardener. So she said to him, 'If you have taken him, tell me where I can go and find him.' And then Jesus spoke a word that turned Mary's world upside down: 'Mary.'

In that moment, hope flooded through her soul and she said, 'Rabboni, Teacher.' She went to hold on to him, to hug him, to embrace him. But Jesus said, 'Stand back. Don't cling to me yet. For I am going to my Father and you need to go back and tell the disciples that I am ascending to my Father and their Father.'

Session 3: The Evidence for the Resurrection

The claim that God raised Jesus from the dead is so extraordinary that we need very good evidence to support it. Historians rarely have complete proof about the circumstances about which they write—rather they have a mixture of credible witnesses and circumstantial evidence. And it is exactly the same when we come to the resurrection of Jesus. Nowhere does anyone try to tell us *how* it happened—rather they talk about the *consequences* of the resurrection. They tell us about the empty tomb, about the resurrection appearances to the disciples, about changes that took place in those disciples and about the experience of Christians down the years.

The earliest record of the resurrection comes in Paul's first letter to the Corinthians, chapter 15, written before the Gospels. In it he writes, 'I passed on to you what was most important and what had also been passed on to me. Christ died for our sins, just as the Scriptures said. He was buried, and he was raised from the dead on the third day, just as the Scriptures said. He was seen by Peter and then by the Twelve. After that, he was seen by more than 500 of his followers at one time, most of whom are still alive, though some have died. Then he was seen by James and later by all the apostles. Last of all, as though I had been born at the wrong time, I also saw him'. Paul stresses four things that he considers of the greatest importance.

- That Jesus died
- That Jesus was buried
- That Jesus was raised to life on the third day, and
- That Jesus appeared to his disciples

He tells us about appearances that are also recorded in the Gospels, like the appearance to Peter, and about some, like the appearance to James, that are only recorded in his letters. One of the most striking characteristics is that time after time the disciples are taken by surprise. Mary thinks Jesus is the gardener. The two disciples on the road to Emmaus do not recognise him, though they have walked with him for several miles. The disciples in the upper room are terrified and think they have seen a ghost. One thing is very clear: the disciples were not expecting Jesus to be raised from the dead. We hear that even when they had seen him, the next time he appeared they needed convincing all over again. These accounts have a ring of truth about them. The disciples became the leaders of the early church. If they had been making up the stories about the resurrection, surely they would have shown their leaders in a better light, as believing all along that Jesus would rise from the dead. They would have shown them as men and women full of faith and confident witnesses of the resurrection. Instead we see them as doubting, fearful—needing to be convinced that the impossible really had happened. They needed to know that it was Jesus, that they hadn't seen a ghost. The obvious authenticity of the resurrection appearances is one piece of evidence for the truth of the resurrection.

One of the other things that some people say is that Jesus didn't really die in the first place. Somehow or other he managed to survive the beatings and the crucifixion, to fool the soldiers who were expert executioners, to survive the sword stuck in his side, and then in the coolness of the tomb to revive, to get out of the grave clothes, to move the stone, and later in the day to convince the disciples, not that he had revived, but that he had actually risen from the dead. When we know what Jesus went through, perhaps that explanation is far more incredible than what Christians believe to be the better explanation of the evidence—that Jesus really was raised from the dead.

There are other suggestions that are sometimes offered to explain the resurrection: for instance that the authorities moved the body to stop the tomb becoming a place of pilgrimage, or that the disciples suffered mass hysteria and convinced themselves that they were encountering the risen Christ, and they weren't. Unfortunately these explanations do not do justice to the evidence: they all raise more questions than they answer.

We have thought about the empty tomb and the resurrection appearances. There are two more pieces of evidence that we need to consider.

- The transformation that happened to the disciples—from a bunch of frightened men and women who locked themselves away for fear that what happened to Jesus could happen to them, to confident people for whom the resurrection was the key point of their preaching. They were prepared to suffer imprisonment, beating, even death, rather than deny the resurrection of Christ.

- The experience of Christians down the ages. This piece of evidence is of a different order. There are many men and women who have come to believe that Jesus was raised from the dead—not simply from the biblical evidence but because of their own experience. They believe that they know Jesus, not just as a historical reality, but as a present, real person. That knowledge of Jesus makes a real difference to their lives. They begin to share now in resurrection life, to experience forgiveness, peace and the transformation that those first disciples knew. Perhaps you may know people like that.

Christians believe that the combination of the empty tomb, the appearances to the disciples, the transformation that took place in those same disciples and the testimony of Christian men and women down the ages is credible evidence for the resurrection. But each person has to weigh it up for themselves.

Session 5: The Gifts of the Spirit

You have been hearing about those beautiful fruits of the Spirit: love and joy and peace and patience and kindness and self-control and so on, and they're given to us by the Holy Spirit so that we can produce the character of Jesus within ourselves. But now we move on to something slightly different, and that is the gifts of the Holy Spirit. And they are given to us to help us to reproduce the ministry of Jesus. Now, he spent his time healing people, delivering them from evil, and always having that clear insight into people's hearts, which was such a hallmark of his ministry. And so, in short, the gifts of the Spirit are given to us so that we can perform some of the ministry of Jesus in the world today.

Now, there are many passages in the Gospels and the Book of Acts which describe this ministry, many different places where the gifts of the Spirit are mentioned. But I want to look particularly at one famous passage in 1 Corinthians, chapter 12, where nine specific gifts are listed. I'm going to read from verse 4. 'There are different kinds of spiritual gifts, but the same Spirit is the source of them all. There are different kinds of service, but we serve the same Lord. God works in different ways, but it is the same God who does the work in all of us.'

Well, you might have noticed the emphasis there on serving. The gifts of the Spirit are not trophies for us to boast about or even toys for us to play with. They are tools for us to use. You might think of a toolbox. You get it out. In my case you probably dust it off, and you use the tools you need for a particular job. So a screwdriver isn't much use if what you need is a hammer, and if the nail doesn't go straight in you need some pliers to pull it out. Well, it's a bit like that with the Holy Spirit. He gives us appropriate gifts for each particular task.

So let's have a look at the gifts as they are listed in this passage. First, there is the gift of wisdom or wise advice. I think this is probably one of the most common of all the gifts, but it can easily go unrecognized in the Christian life. Perhaps you've heard someone say, 'I found myself saying just the right word. It was almost as though it didn't come from me.' Well, under God, that is the gift of wisdom. Being able to help someone with just the right words at a particular time. Very closely allied with this is the gift of knowledge—little pieces of information which when given help you to minister for Christ. It doesn't mean God will tell you everything you need to know about something. But sometimes these divine insights unlock a situation, particularly if it means someone you're praying with realizes that God had to have inspired your words. I was once praying with someone and really felt I should ask them first about their childhood. It turned out they were actually quite angry and then said if I'd suggested praying about anything else, they might have left the building there and then. As we continued, I felt somehow I should also ask them about their name and then perhaps strangely, as this was October, about their celebration of Christmas. But it turned out that these three things together were all deeply connected for them and the very area for which they wanted prayer. Now, I genuinely don't think that I suggested those three topics because of some happy coincidence. I really believe that God was prompting me so that this other person was reminded of the depth of his love for them.

Next is the gift of faith. Now, this needs a bit of explanation because Christians, by definition, have faith in Jesus Christ as Lord. But this is faith for a particular situation at a particular time. Sometimes it's linked with the gift of healing, but often it's for another kind of situation in one's own life. In times of great confusion and uncertainty, it's a gift whereby you just know that God is there, that God is in it. I may not be able to see the road ahead, but I can step forward because of the faith that sustains me. In other words, in the midst of situations of chaos or uncertainty, it's a gift that brings God's peace.

Another gift is the gift of healing. Now, this gift has been rediscovered in many churches in recent years, but of course, it's always been a central part of the gospel. And there have been instances of healing recorded throughout the history of the church. Sometimes it's simply someone praying for somebody else. Sometimes it's allied with the laying on of hands or anointing with olive oil, as in the New Testament. And there are plenty of times when such healings have then been medically verified. But we also know that not everyone is healed. A picture I find helpful is to imagine Jesus walking along the lanes of Galilee. People would come and bring their sick friends and relatives and lay them down on the verges of the lanes so that as Jesus passed by, he would see them. Our responsibility is to bring people to Christ, as it were to place them where he can see them. We do this in prayer and then it's his responsibility as to what happens next, not ours. And very often we need to trust God with these uncertain and difficult situations.

Now, the next gift, I suspect, if you've already looked ahead in the passage, is probably not one which you think you've already got, the power to perform miracles. But let's set this one in context. Have you ever had a prayer answered? Even in a small way that's an example of the kingdom breaking into a world that without such prayer would not have the hope of the gospel in that particular situation. Often, I think, as people find their prayers are answered, so it seems as though there has been a series of these holy coincidences or God-instances. They are the sort of things that bring people into closer relationship with God and help us to trust him. And some people, of course, do have amazing stories to share of the outright miracles they've seen God perform.

The sixth gift is that of speaking God's message, often called prophecy. Some people are particularly gifted in this—in knowing what the will of God is and then proclaiming it, whatever the cost. Now, that can be an official-sounding, 'Thus saith the Lord' kind of prophecy, but very often it's a suggestion, an idea, a proposal that seems to have the touch of the Holy Spirit about it. And as with any gift in the New Testament, it needs to be tested. Just because somebody says 'Thus says the Lord' doesn't mean it is. That's why words of prophecy should be considered by the gathered church so that what's right within a prophecy is distinguished from what's merely a human idea.

Then the gift of discernment, or as the New Living Translation of the Bible puts it, 'the ability to discern whether a message is from the Spirit of God or from another spirit.' Sometimes this is to discern the presence of evil. But I think much more often it's about discerning the way in which the will of God is going, the way in which God is leading through uncertain circumstances. That's why it's a gift so needed by Christian leaders. Very often the questions which come up when decisions are needed are not between good and obvious evil, it's between what is good, and there are often many good things, and what is right, what God actually wants his people to do.

And then lastly, tongues and the interpretation of tongues, or as our passage puts it, 'the ability to speak in unknown languages while another is given the ability to interpret what's being said.' When I was training for ministry, a mentor called this the church's best kept secret. And I think many Christians who use this gift do so in private devotional prayer more than in public where an interpretation is expected. For me, the significance of this gift is the way that it deepens my sense of connection with God. I don't have to think about the words I'm forming with my lips. Rather, it really is a heart-to-heart connection.

Well, obviously there is a whole lot more that could be said about any one of these gifts of the Spirit. And I hope that now you will have a chance to discuss your own response. As you do, bear in mind that they are not trophies to boast about or toys to play with. They are tools given by God to be used in his service for the good of other people.

Resources for you and your Church from

DAVID 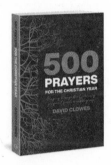 COOK

transforming lives together

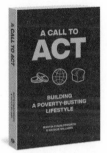

A Call to Act

A practical tool for individual, churches, and small groups, and incorporating discussion questions and accompanying videos, A Call to Act demonstrates that, in order to engage with poverty and need, we must re-evaluate our own attitudes and adopt a poverty-busting lifestyle.

RELEASED: *SEPTEMBER 2020* **PRICE:** *£11.99* **ISBN:** *9780830780686*

500 Prayers for the Christian Year

Written in accessible 'non-Churchy' language, and with prayers based on the Bible readings for every Sunday of all three years of the Lectionary, plus all major Christian holidays.

RELEASED: *OCTOBER 2020* **PRICE:** *£11.99* **ISBN:** *9780830782468*

'40 Prayers' series

Designed to be affordable, accessible, and portable, each volume contains 40 prayers for use either during a specific season in the Christian calendar, key areas of resource for Churches, or for particular seasons of life.

40 PRAYERS FOR ADVENT *9780830782307*
40 PRAYERS FOR THE CHRISTMAS SEASON *9780830782314*
40 PRAYERS FOR ALL-AGE WORSHIP *9780830782321*
40 PRAYERS FOR YOUR QUIET TIME *9780830782338*

RELEASED: *OCTOBER 2020* **PRICE:** *£4.99*

Mission Shaped Living

More than just a tool box of 'how to do evangelism,' over eight sessions Mission Shaped Living will build spiritual practices, vision, hope, and confidence into your life so that sharing God's love with others becomes a joy and not a burden.

LEADER'S GUIDE: £8.99   **PARTICIPANT'S GUIDE: £9.99**
ISBN: 9780830781812   *ISBN: 9780830781805*

RE**SOURCE**

Alive in the Spirit and Active in Mission

ReSource for Anglican Renewal Ministries helps little, local and ordinary churches to engage with the Holy Spirit for renewal, discipleship and mission.

ReSource's vision is for churches of all traditions, shapes and sizes to be alive in the Spirit and active in mission.

"ReSource were excellent! Biblical depth alongside openness to the Holy Spirit and relevant to ordinary church life and my calling to ministry. Real and Honest. Inspiring and refreshing"

Get in touch

ReSource works on the ground locally, to serve churches and support church leaders. **For more information about Renewal events, Church weekends, Sanctuary Days, the Alongside companionship scheme and online Resources Hub visit:**

www.resource-arm.net or contact
ReSource, Meeting Point House, Telford, TF3 4HS,
or **office@resource-arm.net**